THE FACADE
OF
DEMOCRACY

Fijian Struggles For Political Control

1830-1987

A. Ravuvu

Published by
Reader Publishing House
2nd Floor, Procera House,
Suva—Fiji 1991

ISBN 982-227-001-1

Typeset by Word Com, Suva
Text set in 11/12½ Berner
Index by Judith Vuniyaro
Printed by Oceania Printers Ltd, Suva

CONTENT

FOREWORD

Ratu Sir Penaia K. Ganilau *GCMG, KCVO, KBE,*
KStJ,DSO, ED

Professor Asesela Ravuvu, a prominent Fijian academic and anthropologist asked me to contribute a foreword for his new book, "The Facade of Democracy, Fijian Struggles for Political Control 1830-1987".

A number of books on the Fijian socio-economic situation have appeared, since the political upheaval in Fiji 1987—the final year covered in Ravuvu's historical perspective. But his contributions in this book are, I believe, the first serious attempt by a Fijian writer to interpret the political and socio-economic events from Fiji's heyday of colonial rule to independence and parliamentary rule, within the Commonwealth of Nations in 1970, to the two coup d'etats and the declaration of Fiji as a Republic in 1987. These events led to Fiji's expulsion from the Commonwealth of Nations and the unchiefly severance of its treasured links with the British Crown.

I have been deeply involved in the political life of Fiji over some part of the period covered in this book. I was in the crossfire and at the receiving end of the events of 1987 and their aftermath. I do not wish ever to be in that situation again.

Whilst some may not agree with the author's interpretation of some of the events and policies over the century and a half covered in his book, his views nevertheless reflect, in the main, the Fijian viewpoint. The book therefore offers a different perspective and I commend it to all those interested in understanding Fiji's contemporary situation.

The first chapter deals with the period leading up to Cession. It argues that the Fijian chiefs were coerced into ceding Fiji to the British Crown and but for the sensitivity of some earlier colonial administrators to the customs and thinking of the Fijian people, Fijian interests may not have been safeguarded. Ravuvu also argues that Fijian values were constantly under threat in the colonial period from contacts with European civilisation, technology and religion.

Chapter two describes early colonial rule, the resistance by Fijians, particularly the Hill Tribes (Colo people), and the use of force to bring them under control. Ravuvu argues that this eroded Fijian self respect. Fijians became dependent on their traditional leaders and the British administrators to protect their heritage.

The Indian demand for equality and political ascendancy is described in chapter three, which also examines the Fijian fear of Indianisation. This chapter introduces the Salisbury Despatch as the charter of Indian political rights, as it largely influenced the British Government into allowing Indians who went to the Colonies to settle permanently and be treated as full citizens. Their political position was enhanced by their improved economic status, and their demand for common roll started way back in 1933—and continued to Independence in 1970 and beyond.

Chapter four examines sociocultural factors contributing to misunderstanding; the different characteristics, customs and traditions which impact on social interactions between the various communities in Fiji. It also describes the political impasse created by the Fijian desire for paramountcy in their land and the Indian insistence on equal rights under the banner of democracy which the author argues is a guise, their real desire being for political and economic dominance. He suggests that when power changed hands from the Fijian dominated Alliance Government to the Indian dominated Coalition in May 1987, the Fijians had had enough, and that the civil disobedience staged by the Fijians, openly displaying their dislike of the Labour/National Federation Party Coalition, would have ended in a bloodbath had it not been for the bloodless military intervention to prevent it.

The concluding chapter asks, what went wrong? The author identifies a number of reasons. But the reader should be warned that he does not take one side or the other lest the book lose its most important contribution, that of identifying many of the conflicting factors at work in our multiracial society and the complexity of the various issues involved for those who hold leadership positions in Fiji. This book is a positive contribution to our understanding of a Fijian perspective of our contemporary situation. It is also a testimony to the ability of the people of Fiji, post cession and independence, to live together in harmony and with unity in our multifaceted diversity, compared to many other parts of the world in our time. Let us keep it that way for the sake of our future generations and move away from the politics of confrontation in favour of cooperation for the sake of the country we call our home.

PREFACE

The Fijians, the indigenous people of Fiji, do not generally communicate in writing. They listen, observe and communicate verbally among themselves. Thus their feelings and aspirations are seldom communicated to the non-Fijian public or international readers. Being verbally transmitted, their beliefs, feelings and aspirations are usually regarded as transitory, not seriously considered in the long term, and often forgotten. Fortunately for the Fijians, since first contact with the Europeans, some of their feelings, characteristics, and beliefs have been recorded in writing. It is unfortunate, however, that writings about Fijians' feelings and aspirations are not known to the public at large, for they are often kept in archives and museums where only specialists can view them.

An unwritten aspiration of most Fijians on the eve of constitutional independence in 1970 was to be in full control again in their country. It still is.

Their ancestor chiefs were caught in a position in which they had little option but to cede their country to Great Britain in 1874, to be protected from the encroachment of both Tongans and Europeans. By 1970 their grandchildren hoped that at independence they would have the power back in their hands and decide their future destiny. This expectation was not fulfilled for they had to negotiate as only one party in a four-way struggle (the British Government, Fijians, Indians, and other races). They could not get a constitution which recognised their autochthonous position and guaranteed indigenous rights, and gave them power to rule in their country and determine their own destiny.

This 1970 constitution provided for power sharing with other races. Fijians and Indians were given an equal number of seats in Parliament. Furthermore, the constitution preserved many colonial social, economic and political structures that did not harmonize with existing traditional Fijian cultures. The constitution also allowed others who were smart enough and familiar with the economic, social and political systems left behind by the Colonial Government, to exploit them for their further advancement. This was in contrast to the rather reluctant or ambivalent attitudes among Fijians to be fully involved in such foreign systems.

Over twelve books have been written about the 1987 coup d'etats in Fiji, and more are yet to come. All have been very subjective, and almost all negative about the events. This is understandable since most of the authors are immigrants or foreigners. Some of them have found living in Fiji so good for so long that they found the two coups threatening to their superior status. Some have misused their freedom to enhance their individual interests at the expense of the minority, and in particular the indigenous people, and object now that the indigenous people protest effectively.

Fijians have lost the influence and recognition they once enjoyed. Under the facade of "democracy" and "equality of opportunity", immigrants have secured for themselves many diverse positions in the country. They dominate the commercial sector, the professions, the public services and higher education. They emphasise equal opportunity and individual rights, often without realising that they may be depriving Fijians of their inherited rights. Many also counteract or undermine any move for positive discrimination to help Fijians who are lagging behind to achieve real equality of wealth, education, health and welfare. "Democracy" to many immigrants and their descendants in Fiji is a panacea. Decision making by majority rule, equality, and individual freedom have become slogans for maintaining and advancing their interests without realising that these principles are often mutually antagonistic. Majority rule can turn into the rule of prejudice and the power of many to violate the rights of the few. Democratic decision making procedures by no means guarantee the best decisions. In some circumstances the best decisions come from entrusting the responsibility to make them to a few well-meaning and knowledgeable people. The renowned British Prime Minister, Winston Churchill, once remarked that "democracy is the worst system devised by the wit of man, except for all others".

Most people today tend to view democracy as the solution to every problem. They assume that when the democratic principle is established in a society, that society will become an ideal place to live. They view democracy as a system in which the will of the majority always prevails. Thus they insist on majority rule even in situations where other principles might serve as well or better, and anyone who opposes is condemned as "undemocratic".

For Fiji, 14 May 1987 was a turning point when self determination was reintroduced by revolutionary means. The two military coups of May and September of 1987 received the overwhelming support of most Fijians with the exception of those few whose power had been abolished by the takeovers.

Real self determination has now begun to emerge in Pacific states. They are now freeing themselves from the remaining shackles of colonialism which continue to belittle Pacific cultures, stunt initiatives, discourage new economic and political alignments and the freedom to make choices in dealing with one's own destiny.

The Fijian leaders in 1990 adopted a new constitution which provides them with a better opportunity to control their country and to be ruled in a more culturally appropriate way and at the same time protect human rights and justice for every person living in Fiji. Fiji is not the only country which has revised its constitution. Vanuatu, the Solomon Islands, Papua New Guinea, and the Cook Islands among others have done so, and are now considering more changes to make their constitutions fit better into Pacific cultures.

The purpose of this book is to provide a historical perspective of Fijian struggles to maintain control over their land and people and to achieve independence from externally derived domination. It shows that Fijians have all along suffered from pressure from non-Fijians. It is a history of Fijians trying to defend themselves against being controlled by outsiders. It looks at the 1987 coups, not as events in isolation, but also considers other factors which have been ignored by other writers and which culminated in the two military takeovers of the government. It is hoped that this book will provide another side of the story and a better understanding of why Colonel (now Major General) Sitiveni Rabuka acted as he did and why, in doing so, he received the overwhelming support of the Great Council of Chiefs, the highest forum pertaining to Fijian affairs.

GLOSSARY

colo	interior of the big island
draunikau	exuvia magic
kaicolo	hillmen
koro	village
lotu	religion
mataqali	sub-lineage or sub-clan
matetaka levu	measles epidemic
meke	Fijian traditional dance
raikoro	inspection of village
soro	make atonement
tabua	whale's teeth
taukei	indigenous or owner
taukei ni vanua	owners of the land
Tui Viti	King of Fiji
turaga ni Bolatagane	gentlemen from Great Britain
vanua	tribe and locality
vulagi	visitor or foreigner

CHAPTER ONE

Encroachment of European Politics

Local politics before 1874

The Fijian people lived in kin groups which were generally independent and autonomous, with tenuous, political connection with each other. Mutual suspicion and fear generally kept them apart. They developed a sense of guardedness in approaching and interacting with one another, when that was essential. Groups varied in size, but were generally fairly small. Membership was fluid, allowing dissenters to break away and form their own groups and establish themselves in various localities, not too close to be harassed and not too distant to receive help from their kin when needed. Each group was known by the name of the locality upon which it established dwellings. Groups moved about, integrated and disintegrated according to the perceived advantages of leaders and members alike, especially when individual freedom and control over one's destiny was severely threatened. Where the recognition and respect of individual or group identity and worth had been ignored or eroded, group solidarity was likely to be challenged or weakened, irrespective of the kinds of force used to maintain it. Thus intrigues, plots and counter plots all became a means of either maintaining or debasing one's recognition and identity. Control of one's destiny and the maintenance of one's identity have always been a central focus for Fijians and they still are the central elements in Fijian political struggles.

Because of the fluidity of the ancient Fijian social and political systems, many independent tribal groups and chiefs were often at loggerheads for one reason or another. Land, women, and insult to chiefs were three main causes of wars. It was evident from the writings of early explorers, traders and missionaries who visited and worked in Fiji from the early mid 19th century that the rule of the Fijian chief was generally despotic. But the chief who did not adequately care for his followers could instigate his own destruction by those who were not happy with his rule, or by someone else whose assistance they requested through offerings and gifts. The political system was generally in a state of flux, so no one political grouping was forever dominant.

Increasing contact with traders in sandalwood and later beche-de-mer (in the 1830's and 1840's) greatly influenced the existing political situation and enabled a number of chiefs to consolidate and extend their power and influence over a much wider area than ever before particularly in coastal areas. The trade, generally through chiefs, was mostly a barter of muskets and iron tools for the local produce. Through the use of firearms, runaway sailors, and the assistance of trading ship captains vying for cargoes, chiefs like Ratu Naulivou and others saw the advantages of being helpful to and closely associated with the source of the new technology. Such chiefs were able to enhance their position and to influence other chiefs and their people.

About the year 1820, Bau, through its chief, Ratu Naulivou, became the centre of political power in Fiji, its influence being acknowledged in many parts of the Fiji Group. Although various social groups were expected to pay homage and tribute to Bau, they were not under servitude in the enslavement sense of the word. These units had a well defined system of political relationship which determined the position and the role the different groups held and played with respect to each other, including the extent and degree of obeisance which each group rendered to its superior. The chief of the most influential or superior unit often gathered around him chiefs of subordinate groups who acted as advisers. They also served to check the exercise of his power.

It was not unusual to play off one chief against another, and smaller weaker groups often exploited the situation by favouring those who could provide them with the best security and advantages. Alliances through marriage and other social and political ties were not infrequent and often exploited for supra-familial activities such as the staging of large ceremonial exchanges of offerings or gifts, and the subduing of common opponents or despotic chiefs. Each group had kinship and tributary relations with almost every other group and this extended as more social interaction occurred through the influences of Christian missionaries and the presence of foreign powers with superior technology.

Although coastal chiefs like those of Bau and Rewa did appreciate the advantages of the presence of some Europeans amongst them, they were quick to become revengeful if their plans were thwarted or if Europeans did not comply or were not useful to their causes. For example, Ratu Cakobau, in 1844, ordered the European community out of Levuka when they did not secure him something worth purchasing from the goods salvaged from Charlie Pickering's cutter which was wrecked near Cicia, in Lau. Instead, some Levuka Europeans helped Pickering to escape with the goods to Rewa. They retreated to Solevu in Vanua Levu, but did not stay there long before Ratu Cakobau, in 1849, again asked them to return to Levuka. Whites thus gained some understanding of their usefulness and importance to the chiefs. From then onwards Europeans, and Tongans, started to act more independently in their own interests *(Routledge, 1985, p. 69)*.

Fijian chiefs however, continued to be very vigilant and cautious, and became suspicious of any move which they thought would reduce their authority and thus control over their people and land. As long as Europeans complied with their demands, they were acceptable, even invaluable.

Erosion of chiefly power

Threats to the authority and independence of Fijian chiefs to decide their own people's destinies began to be felt strongly during the 1830's, when European traders and consular agents of metropolitan powers began to establish themselves permanently in the country and work independently for their own self-interests.

The Tongans and missionaries added extra dimensions to outside encroachment upon chiefly authority. Tongan warriors and canoe-builders had either weakened or strengthened the position of some chiefs, aligning themselves with those from whom they could get the greatest advantage. Some supported Bau: others with the Tui Cakau, and through marriage links with chiefly families in Bau, Lakeba, Nadroga, Lau, Cakaudrove and elsewhere. Tongan influence and threat became a force to be reckoned with in the struggle for political ascendancy and dominance among Fijian chiefs. Working closely with the Christian missionaries, Tongans established themselves in Lau and made alliances with other parts of Fiji. The spread of Christianity throughout Fiji was often equated with Tongan scheming for political aggrandizement.

Chiefs like Ratu Cakobau found this suspicious and unpalatable at times. It was a dilemma difficult to resolve without losing out politically in the end. To be or not to be Christian was the question which confronted Ratu Cakobau and other chiefs. In the end they succumbed in order to acquire the support and recognition of the Tongans, Europeans, missionaries, naval officers, and consular agents who had the political leverage supported by foreign powers interested in the safety and security of their nationals and traders living among Fijians. Through a number of circumstances Ratu Cakobau was recognised as the *Tui Viti* (King of Fiji), a status and recognition which made him politically vulnerable to, and manipulated by, Europeans who aspired to control Fiji and to bring it under the protection of either Britain or the United States, which were concerned to protect and enhance their own interests.

Intimidated by American commanders for not paying damages claimed by American traders for which he was unjustifiably blamed, King Cakobau felt that he had no choice but to cede Fiji to Great Britain; a view strengthened by the advice of the British consular agent, Pritchard. He had to do this if he were to retain and reaffirm his position as *Tui Viti* and at the same time secure protection against outside encroachment which would further undermine his authority and control. Fijian chiefs were led to believe that neither their power nor their positions would be changed by ceding Fiji to Britain. Britain, however, rejected the initial offer.

Coastal chiefs were regarded suspiciously by chiefs of the interior of Viti Levu who also resisted any effort to convert them to Christianity. To be converted implied subservience to Bau, so any attempt to influence them in the name of the chief of Bau was strongly resisted. This was a factor in the killing of the Reverend Thomas Baker on 21 July, 1867. The missionaries and the British consular agents urged Ratu Cakobau to punish the *kai colo* (hillmen) for the murder. Although the Bau chief was reluctant to confront the *kai colo* over whom he had little control, he had to act if he was to retain his influence and authority inherent in the title of *Tui Viti*. Unfortunately the expedition led by Ratu Cakobau was ambushed by the Noemalu people at Vatukubu in the upper Wainimala River, and Ratu Cakobau had to return to safety, leaving the *colo* people alone unmolested for some time.

The influx of Europeans, especially in 1870, added another dimension to the *Tui Viti's* problems of trying to contain outsiders who were eager to make quick wealth and to acquire land. Generally these newcomers defied any effort to maintain law and order as this would restrict their freedom to ruthlessly and fraudulently grab Fijian natural resources, particularly land. Earlier arrivals who had established themselves and acquired properties, however, wanted law and order and were generally against any effort to subdue the warlike Fijians, fearing retaliation from them.

As more land was taken over by the white settlers, free access through such areas by Fijians became increasingly restricted or impossible. European interference had been strongly felt as settler numbers increased. Ruling chiefs realised that their traditional authority was becoming ever more restricted. European planters formed societies to protect their interests and, together with other white settlers, attempted to acquire the assistance of some Fijian chiefs like Ratu Cakobau and Ma'afu to establish some form of government.

Fijian chiefs were constantly threatened with being taken hostage or annihilated if they did not comply with the demands of the settlers, who usually solicited the assistance of either the US or British naval officers in port. Gun-boat diplomacy was often practised. Routledge noted:

> The time was one of considerable uncertainty. Clearly the ruling chiefs had lost power and were no longer the main protagonists in Fijian political processes. On the other hand, Europeans had tried a range of schemes for the creation of power, and then asked external authorities to take over with equal want of success. The result was that both sides were reduced to recognising that some kind of mixed solution appeared the only one possible. Cakobau's previous experience with European advisers had been far from encouraging, but he was forced to try again .... (*Routledge*, 1985, pp. 124-125).

Among the Fijian chiefs themselves rivalry and competition for power was rife. The Bau chiefs under the leadership of Ratu Cakobau were suspicious of Ma'afu and the Tovata Confederacy, consisting of the Bua, Macuata, Cakaudrove and Lau chiefs. Even among the chiefs of the Tovata confederacy, Ma'afu's authority was only nominal and the chiefs of Vanua Levu continued to assert their own individualities and interests.

Although Ratu Cakobau was generally recognised, particularly by the Europeans, as *Tui Viti* (King of Fiji) he had little control over other chiefdoms outside the traditional boundaries of Bauan influence.

Usurpation of power by Europeans

In such a situation the need for an established form of government was urgent. Encouraged by a small group of European settlers, Ratu Cakobau, supported by a number of chiefs including Ma'afu, established in 1871 a constitutionally formed government, although Ratu Cakobau came to be a figurehead who reigned but hardly ruled. Although it was popularly known as the "Cakobau government," decisions were made by Europeans who dominated the cabinet and who expected the Fijians to contribute an equal share of the revenue without equally complementary benefits. For instance, every Fijian male was levied with an annual poll tax of five dollars, and of at least a dollar for females.

> Apart from this, the men were also liable to a labour tax of two days a month, worked out on development work of some kind, 'provided that this shall not exempt the inhabitants from planting of food, the building of houses, etc'. A scheme of government plantation was later initiated to provide the opportunity to pay off these obligations. This was an unjust provision, but there was a worse. Planters employing men who owed the labour tax were able to commute it for eight cents a day if they did not want to lose their labourers' services ... Labourers themselves, on the other hand, were able to commute only at the rate of twelve cents a day. (*Routledge*, 1985, p.134).

There was a great deal of criticism and even antagonism towards the Ratu Cakobau Government. Much more was spent on the salaries of officers running the government than on the means for providing services. Of $120,000 collected in one year, $77,000 were spent on salaries (*Routledge*, 1985, p. 134.) The lack of cash was a major factor in the European traders and planters' dissatisfaction with the government; and the amount of revenue collected often fell short of expectations. The situation was made more difficult by the lack of support for the government from the British consul, who regarded it as an encroachment upon his administrative domain. He criticised every action of the government as arbitrary, and together with others condemned the hiring out of the subdued or vanquished Fijians to European planters as a means of keeping under control and at the same time acquiring government revenue. The Wesleyan missionaries and Marist priests also opposed the excessive taxation of their Fijian wards. "The revenue raised, in total and from the Fijians alone, was very similar in quantity to that raised by the colonial government; and that was less, per head of population, than anywhere else in the empire." (*Routledge*, 1985, p. 147).

Through the efforts and understanding of such European settlers like R.S. Swanston, the Minister of Native Affairs, and D. Wilkinson, W.S.

Carew, A Forbes, and J.L.C. Payne, acting as provincial secretaries in Bua, Rewa, Kadavu and Tailevu respectively, the Fijians in those areas were made amenable to the intentions of the government. They understood traditional Fijian politics, and all had sympathy for the Fijian cause and were determined to protect Fijians from unscrupulous European planters. In 1872, Wilkinson became a Native Commissioner looking after the problems of the administration of a number of provinces. (Wilkinson and Carew, being so well versed in Fijian customs, later became the first land claim commissioners investigating and recording the Fijian land tenure system during the early period of the colonial government).

Through the influence of these officials and in particular of Swanston, the integrity of Fijian society and the structure of authority within the various chiefdoms continued to be maintained as the basis for the new administration. The high chiefs were made to play as big a part as possible in the administration of their own people.

The Ratu Cakobau government was supported in the provinces of Tailevu, Naitasiri, Rewa, Namosi, Serua and Kadavu. The Macuata chiefs were not supportive of the government due mainly to an internal power struggle among the two prominent chiefs, Ratu Ritova and Ratu Katonivere. Bua also gave its support to the new government only after Mr Forbes and the *Tui Bua* travelled about and explained to the people the purposes of the government. In 1873, the Nadroga and the Nasigatoka chiefs declared their support for the Ratu Cakobau Government. Ba, where the traditional authority structure was more fragmented than anywhere else except in the interior, and where European settlers lived in fear of hostile natives and showed contempt for the Levuka based government for not giving them any protection, took longer to accept the government and pay taxes. The willingness to pay taxes and recognise the government came about in 1872, only after an expedition of armed constabulary from Levuka arrived in Ba to protect the European planters after two of them (James McIntosh and John Spiers), had been killed and several farming families attacked by hostile Fijians. It was only then that the Ba settlers were very appreciative of the protection provided by the government and were willing to pay taxes.

Although the Ratu Cakobau Government had sound legislation for the recruitment and treatment of labour, it was difficult to monitor its implementation. Planters tended to abuse it and local settler magistrates often favoured their contemporaries, so justice was biased towards planter's demands. Payment of fees and wages was irregular, even though employers usually demanded maximum hours of work and the highest productivity.

Moreover, workers were not well fed and were often treated harshly, at times brutally.

Attempts at land alienation

Several attempts were made by the European dominated government of Ratu Cakobau to take land away from Fijian control. For instance, in 1871, a Land Bill was introduced declaring that all land not already used by Europeans should belong to the Crown. This was rejected due to several difficulties and disagreements relating to the continued ownership of land and by planter's demands for more plantation land. Already most coastal arable lands were in European hands with little regard for the Fijian owner's interest. The fear of exciting violence from Fijians and abuse by Europeans discouraged further attempts to pursue this policy. Planters and traders, including the British consul, did not wish to acknowledge the rights of Fijian authorities over the land resource. Planters imposed their own rules even beyond their acquired territories. Fijians were often denied access to the sea, and disallowed from fishing in their own rivers which flowed through or adjacent to lands acquired by Europeans. Plantation labourers were instructed to shoot Fijians on sight and Fijians were often pursued by planters when foraging in nearby bushes. Such restrictions on the free use of their resources angered most Fijians particularly along the river valleys and coastal fringes of the two main islands (Viti Levu and Vanua Levu) occupied by whites. The murder in 1873 of the Burnes family and their 26 labourers at Vunisamaloa in Ba was believed to be in retaliation for such grievances and harsh treatment received by some villagers of the upper Ba River.

Throughout Fiji large blocks of land were bought, quite often without the knowledge of those Fijians occupying them. The inhabitants had to be removed by force and hardly given time to use up their crops which were usually taken over by the European land purchasers. Europeans usually assumed a position of superiority over the Fijians and thus often acted abrasively and condescendingly in dealing with land purchases.

To protect themselves from the requirements of the Ratu Cakobau Government and from Fijian opposition, whites formed an organisation known as the British Subjects' Mutual Protection Society or Ku Klux Klan, with the same racist attitudes and objectives as its American counterpart. The members of this organisation were defiant of the Ratu Cakobau Government. They had not been happy with its oppressive taxation policy and the government's readiness to protect Fijian interests. They demanded that the rights of European settlers and the development of a plantation economy should be made paramount over all other interests, and in particular Fijian interests over their land. Through the assistance of Captain Chapman of the H.M.S. *Dido*, European settlers were advised to cooperate with the Ratu Cakobau government. Thus, the most racist whites were brought to submission and two of their prominent leaders were deported to Australia on board the H.M.S. *Dido*.

Affirmation of centralised authority

A few cabinet ministers in the Ratu Cakobau government such as Swanston and Thurston, though defensive of Fijian interests, were bent on bringing quasi-independent tribal groups of the coastal areas and those of the interior of Viti Levu, under government control. The inland villagers, who were the scourge of white settlers along the river valleys of Wailevu, Nasigatoka, and the Ba River in particular, needed to be organised, administered and brought under the authority of the government, even if it would mean the use of force. A program of systematic centralisation was mounted by the Government, backed by its military forces. Disciplined and well drilled troops with rifles and commanded by experienced officers were far too strong for the club and spear-wielding tribal warriors defending their traditional domain and autonomy. Although King Cakobau's forces were generally superior through the effective use of their firearms, this did not easily bring all the interior people to submission without further resistance. A number of pitched battles were fought before they were made to abandon their inaccessible habitations. Feeling the pressure concentrated upon them, the people of the interior abandoned their inaccessible villages and formerly impregnable fortresses and were forcibly settled in larger villages within the reach of the authority of the government. Then, some of the vanquished, including chiefs, were either sentenced to death or deported to penal servitude on European plantations. Europeans had thus established an arrogant assumption of superiority over Fijians and used every means to bring the Fijians under their control.

On the other hand, Europeans traders and planters not happy with the Ratu Cakobau government urged the government to give up and annex Fiji to Britain. They hoped to enhance their rights and control over Fijian natural resources and the development of a plantation economy. There were also efforts to subvert the government by forcing ministers supporting

Fijian causes and the Ratu Cakobau Government to resign. In the 1873 Assembly, while the Cakobau government were trying to bring the interior tribes under control, these ministers were accused of manipulating government funds and defrauding the revenue for bribery and support. Although the ministers were asked to resign, King Cakobau refused the resignations on the grounds that these ministers were accomplishing a great deal in subduing the unsubmissive tribes of the interior, and that such interruption in the running of the government was not good for the welfare and prosperity of the country.

The beginning of the end of Ratu Cakobau's Government

With a European majority in the Assembly, it was inevitable that European interests would predominate over Fijian affairs. It was firmly believed by some Cabinet Ministers like Thurston, Swanston and others, that for peace and prosperity to prevail, Fijians should have a greater say in the government of their country. Thurston, for instance, informed the governments' representatives in Australia and New Zealand ".... that unless Fijians were assured of their just privileges as the native inhabitants of the country, a race war similar to that of the Maori catastrophe would follow". (*Routledge*, 1985, p. 181)

On the other hand Fijian chiefs in the Assembly were much concerned and confused at the European members' behaviour in relation to the government ministers and their fervent intention to undermine the Ratu Cakobau Government. For instance, Ma'afu told the opposition members of the Assembly that they would be kept out of the house if they did not stop personally abusing the ministers. In a later discussion at Bau, Ma'afu told the commanding officer of the Royal Navy stationed in Australia, Commander Stirling, that:

> . . . When the Missionaries came here, the resident whites told us that Christianity was an evil thing and the missionaries were bad men. But we believed they were wrong and we embraced Christianity and found it to be a good thing. Now we have formed a government because we believe that it will benefit our country and the whites are united in saying that the government is no good, and that the ministers are bad men. They are continually speaking evil of the ministers. They say your kingdom is destroyed everything is over with the government. But we believe in the government. (*Routledge*, 1985, p.181).

By 1873, the number of Europeans in Fiji exceeded 1,800 and the control of political affairs was already in their hands. The Fijian chiefs were merely their puppets. The political situation was becoming intolerable as the Fijian chiefs and their European advisers toiled at maintaining the control and autonomy of the Ratu Cakobau Government against the efforts of other whites trying to destabilise and to annex Fiji unconditionally to Britain for the protection and enhancement of their own interests. Referring to a Fiji correspondent of the Sydney Morning Herald who had written unfavourably of those opposed to Ratu Cakobau's government the *Fiji Times* wrote:

> What he tells us about the King's determination to oppose the annexation movement is of very small moment. The white settlers of Fiji have been and are today the ruling power of the group, and the chiefs and the natives are merely their puppets. What the majority of the settlers demand, that Cakobau must accede to, his autocracy will not go down with white men who have been accustomed to a liberal form of government. He feels the power of the white race, and must bow to it. Already the Anglo-Saxon has firmly planted his foot here, and so certainly must he remain.
>
> The whites can do without the natives, but Fiji can never again be free of the white man. Her destiny is sealed, and as surely as the American Indians, the New Zealanders (Maoris), and the Australians (Aborigines) had to give way to superior race, so surely must the Fijian follow in the same course (*Fiji Times*, 4 January, 1873).

In 1873, the British sent another commission of inquiry under Commodore J.G. Goodenough and E. Layard, who was also to act as consul, to investigate if there was any real necessity to annex Fiji. Strong distrust in the efficiency of the Ratu Cakobau Government and lack of confidence in its ministers as relayed to him by the opposition whites prompted Goodenough to do everything in his power to annex Fiji to Great Britain. On the other hand, Thurston, Chief Secretary of the Ratu Cakobau government, tried to protect the integrity of the government at all costs, in case Fiji and the Fijians were left at the mercy of unscrupulous whites who had been working hard to disrupt Fijian efforts to maintain political control of their own affairs.

Coercion for annexation

On 22 December 1873, Ratu Cakobau was invited on board the H.M.S.

Pearl by Goodenough where he was lectured and even threatened to provide a definite answer to the question of annexing Fiji to Britain. The Commissioners had little liking for Thurston whom the Fijian chiefs trusted. They perceived him as opposed to the further enhancement of European predominance in Fiji, and they tried to make Ratu Cakobau and other chiefs ignore him and do their own negotiation for the government. Although Thurston also believed in the necessity for annexation, he felt it should not be imposed against the will of the chiefs, so he did everything he could to prevent the Commissioners from destroying the Ratu Cakobau Government. The chiefs, having great trust and confidence in Thurston, accepted his advice and refused to make an offer until he advised them that their rights would be protected and paramount. Furthermore, the chiefs distrusted the Commissioners for being too concerned with the whites, who were believed to be conniving with Ma'afu, a Tongan chief, whose loyalty to the Fijian cause was yet to be confirmed.

Forcing the issue of annexation and undermining the efforts of the government, Layard advised Thurston not to promulgate the 1873 constitution which would allow Fijians a greater say in the legislature. He was also warned of being seized and deported for trial in Sydney for his life if things went wrong and that blood would flow. It was obvious that the Europeans were determined to have the country annexed and to deprive the Fijian chiefs of their control over the land and destinies. Thus the Europeans objected to the constitution as a justification for any political violence that might be intended at depriving the independence of the Fijian chiefs so that they would have little choice but to cede their country to Britain. The Commissioners publicly criticised the government as inappropriate to the needs of Fiji with an increasing European population. They even demanded a complete financial statement for the whole period of the government's existence in an effort to substantiate the inefficiency of the government and its ministers. Even Ratu Cakobau and other chiefs were told by the two commissioners that Britain was prepared to take over the government, and that the chiefs should also be aware of the problems that lay ahead as the white population increased. The implication was that the Fijian chiefs were incapable of running the government, while England or Englishmen could.

When Commodore Goodenough was presented with the draft of a deed of cession which focused on maintaining the status and authority of the chiefs and addressing the question of land to the advantage of the Fijians, he became elusive but continued to convey the view that the interests and wishes of the Fijians were of lesser importance than those of Europeans.

There was no doubt the chiefs acted under pressure from Europeans who had bought land which they could not enjoy while it was occupied by Fijians, and for which they wanted registered titles. Areas of land had been sold by chiefs who had not title to them. There were also cases of the same land being sold to two or more buyers. Many of the deeds covering land transactions were never fully understood by the Fijians who signed them, and many land boundaries were not clearly defined.

When on 6 March, 1874, Ratu Cakobau formally informed Goodenough and Layard of his intention to continue with the government under his own name, he was told by the Commodore that England would accept this, but would demand good government which treated European and Fijian equally. He nonetheless showed his strong disapproval when he said that he did not "think well of chiefs who are unable to know their own minds". (*Routledge*, 1985, p.198). He also reminded Ratu Cakobau that the government had been initiated by Europeans for Europeans and that the minister of the government should command the respect of the European community. Goodenough was determined to destroy the government and to force another offer for cession. Both Commissioners did not like to discuss matters with Thurston and ignored him, although he was the only minister of the government trusted by Ratu Cakobau at the time. When Goodenough gathered the chiefs, they were still determined to continue with the government and with Thurston who had been appointed by Ratu Cakobau as the only minister of the government. Goodenough became very authoritarian and paternalistic in his approach. He demanded an answer as to why his advice on cession was not taken and why none of the foreign consuls had been consulted of the formation of a government and the appointment of a minister.

Later on, a heated discussion ensued between Ratu Cakobau and Goodenough, during which Ratu Cakobau questioned the rights of the foreigners to have any voice in the selection of ministers. He emphasised that the country did not belong to foreigners and that the Fijian chiefs had not been taught to give away their country, even though foreigners had taught them how to write. (See *Routledge*, 1985, pp.200-201 for details).

By 20 March, 1874, after a number of confrontations and meetings, the king's special and trusted adviser, Thurston, being under a great deal of pressure from the hostility of the Commissioners and other opposition whites, had little choice but to acquire the cooperation of the Commissioners. He thus advised the chiefs that there was little hope of carrying on with the government without the cooperation of the Commissioners.

In a meeting at the government headquarters at Nasova, Levuka, on 20 March, 1874, Ratu Cakobau informed the commissioners that he and the chiefs of Fiji were prepared to again offer the cession of their islands to Britain. Goodenough accepted and agreed that only the government was being offered, and not the land or the people. This conditional offer of 20 March, 1874 was important from the Fijian point of view. Not agreeable to such an offer with conditions, the British government sent Sir Hercules Robinson, Governor of New South Wales, to negotiate for unconditional cession. It was only then that the Fijian chiefs were pressured to agree to the unconditional cession having been assured by His Excellency that their rights and interests would be recognised as far as might be consistent with British sovereignty. From 20 March onward, the Fijian chiefs had deprived themselves of the full control of their islands, giving it away to an imperial power in which they had to put their confidence and trust to protect themselves from the encroachment of others. Ratu Cakobau was later observed to be depressed and reserved at the unconditional cession, but in the end he agreed. He commented that giving away a thing on conditions was not chieflike.

> If I give a chief a canoe, and he knows that I expect something from him, I do not say, 'I give you this canoe on condition of your only sailing it on certain days, of your not letting such and such a man on it, or of your only using a particular kind of rope with it,' but I give him the canoe right out, and trust to his generosity and good faith to make me the return he knows I expect. If I were to attach conditions, he would say, 'I do not care to be bothered with your canoe, keep it to yourself.' Why should we have any anxiety about the future? What is the future? Britain... If matters remain as they are, Fiji will become like a piece of driftwood on the sea, and be picked up by the first passer-by. The whites who have come to Fiji are a bad lot. They are mere stalkers on the beach ... Of one thing I am assured, that if we do not cede Fiji, the white stalkers on the beach, the cormorants, will open their maws and swallow us. By annexation the two races, white and black will be bound together, and it will be impossible to sever them. The interlacing has come ...; law will bind us together, and the stronger nation will lend stability to the weaker. (*Derrick*, 1950, p.248).

On 28 September, after two days deliberation among the high chiefs, the king, Ratu Cakobau, proclaimed: "We give Fiji unreservedly to the Queen of Britain, that she may rule us justly and affectionately, and that we may live in peace and prosperity". After the Council of Chiefs considered in detail a draft of the terms of cession and approved it, the king and four of the ruling chiefs formally signed the Deed of Cession and toured the islands in the H.M.S. *Pearl* with Sir Hercules Robinson to get the signatures of other high chiefs and brought the chiefs themselves to Levuka for the formal ceremony of the Deed of Cession. On Saturday, 10 October, 1874, the remaining chiefs and Sir Hercules Robinson put their signatures on the Deed of Cession, finalising the beginning of the end of Fijian control over his land and destiny.

Power changed hands

It was obvious from the beginning of Fijian contact with European explorers and traders that the acquisition of Fijian natural resources and their exploitation and development for the use of metropolitan powers were at the centre of European efforts to subjugate by force and colonise by deception. Fear and helplessness of being either subdued, or exterminated from the face of the earth in which their power predominated, forced Fijian chiefs to relegate their control and power and to comply with European suggestions and demands. These chiefs complied reluctantly, being promised that they and their people and land would be protected, because they were under considerable pressure and possible threat, and they believed in the generosity and honesty of their close European advisors. They hoped that the reciprocity they expected would come forth in the form of stable government and the protection of their rights, lands and other property. They thus ceded Fiji with no condition at all. Little did they know what the future held for them, but chose to depend upon the goodwill and wisdom of the new rulers. Their chiefly and Fijian cultural way of giving things away unconditionally but with the quiet expectation of a return equal to or greater than what had been offered has little equivalent in European culture. Thus a cultural misunderstanding occurred when Fiji was ceded unreservedly to Britain.

Britain was left free to govern Fiji as she thought fit. It was only through the understanding of the earlier colonial administrators and their sensitivity to the customs and thinking of the Fijians that the British colonial government paid heed to the necessity of keeping Fijian interests paramount in what was once their native land. From then onward, the future of the Fijian people depended a great deal on the personalities of the colonial administrators and the policies they adopted. Successive British colonial administrators with different socio-economic and political policies, contributed to the various positions and conditions in which the indigenous Fijians had been placed and in relation to other immigrants who have since come to live with them. Fijians since Cession were subjected to colonial rule and made subordinate to its white administrators who usually did their best to impress their wards that they were here to rule, to be respected and obeyed. It was again to be proved to the Fijians that the saying "might is right", reigned amongst all men irrespective of the ideals of equality and justice the so-called "civilized people" purported to believe in and sometimes practise. Vested interests, taking the front of saving and developing the "primitive" race, or commonly known as the "white man's burden", has usually been a driving force behind colonialism. Under the forced acculturation, traditional thoughts, beliefs and practices were strongly denounced, prohibited and even made redundant and inferior by the introduction of European software and hardware. The use of such technology had since been the most effective tool for a people's cultural adaptation and ultimate conversion and assimilation. It has, since first contact with foreign technology, increasingly deprived indigenous Fijians of their capacity to handle their life more meaningfully in the light of what their context could provide. It also made them more dependent on foreigners and migrants who continually emphasised their contributions and indispensability to the development of the people and the country, and thus rights of adoption, and claim for political control and equality.

CHAPTER TWO

Early Colonial Rule and its Aftermath

Resistance to colonial rule.

After cession in 1874, Fijians no longer had absolute control over their own polity, although there were still some dissenters, in particular the chiefs of the interior of the main island of Viti Levu. These people, popularly described by Brewster as the *Hill Tribes of Fiji* (Brewster, 1922) were yet to be formally told that the entire country and its people and land were already under the control of the British Government. After months of delicate negotiations between Walter Crew, representing the new government, and the inland tribes of Viti Levu, 69 chiefs and their retainers agreed to meet government representatives at Navuso on 22 January, 1875. They were then told by the government administrator Mr. E.L. Layard that Fiji had been ceded to Britain and that they should cooperate with and be loyal to the new ruling power. After the meeting, five of the most prominent chiefs accompanied the official party to Levuka in order to pay homage to Ratu Cakobau. On 25 January they visited Ratu Cakobau at Draiba, on the next day visited the H.M.S. *Dido* from which they caught measles. All were to die, and the chiefs returning home carried death with them. Between February and March, this measles epidemic, or the *matetaka levu* as it was known to the Fijians, ravaged the country and drastically reduced its population. The Fijians began to wonder what the new era had in stock for them. Suspicion and superstition were reactivated, and many people blamed their conversion to Christianity and disobedience and disloyalty to their traditional leaders and gods as causes.

17

Several tribes in various ways and degrees began resisting the evangelising effort of the Christian missionaries and thus delaying the establishment and extension of the British rule and authority amongst them. The uprising of certain *colo* tribes against colonial authority in 1876 was a manifestation of such resistance and of their continued assertion of independence. Chiefs were often appeased and their loyalty reinforced by the presentation of gifts from government officials. Writing from Nasaucoko on 16 February, 1876, the Resident Commissioner of Colo, Walter Carew, informed the Colonial Secretary, N.E. Havelock, of events in his area of jurisdiction:

> . . . Immediately after the arrival at our camp of Kolikoli (a chief of Colo) to inform us of his intention to be loyal to the government, I had a visit from Nabiri, the chief of Matanibilalevu on the Wainavau creek on and near which are situated several villages whose people I believed to be faithful to their professions of loyalty made at Navuso last year.
> He came by a circuitous route to inform me that they all intended to remain faithful to the government and after a long conversation I dismissed him with a small present for himself and the chief of Vunatawa (CSO File 76/436).

Fijian chiefs were generally unhappy that their "once despotic" authority had been curtailed by the presence of the colonial government. Now and then they would reassert their authority by disobeying certain arbitrary orders of the colonial administrators, to show that they were still in command of their own people. On the other hand the colonial administrators had to show that they were here to rule and to be obeyed and respected. This had to be demonstrated in action. It was not unusual for many of them to display a condescending attitude and arrogance towards Fijian people, and to be in turn despotic and arbitrary, harsh and severe in handling Fijian affairs. Advising the Colonial Secretary of an action he had taken, Mr Carew, the first Rresident Commissioner of Colo (interior of Viti Levu) wrote:

> . . . I have written to Nacanikalou (chief of the Vatusila people) and to Buli Matailobau giving the former permission to reoccupy his tribal land subject to the consent of His Excellency the Governor but I have ordered him to build his village on a site called Naivucini, on the lowland near the river and not to put up any defensive works or rebuild on a hill top at a place called Nacau.
> To the Buli Matailobau I have issued orders not to interfere for the future with these people . . . (CSO File 76/325).

Chiefs and people who disobeyed orders by government officials were usually severely dealt with. They were either put under custody or deported to other remote and foreign areas in Fiji away from sight and support of their kinsmen. Some were placed in European plantations to work out their penalties, and some were tried and executed. For instance, on 28 August, 1878, Walter Carew, wrote to the Colonial Secretary requesting approval to deport a Fijian by the name of Tete:

> . . . My reason for requesting his deportation was for disobedience to the express orders of Sir Authur Gordon occupying the position of supreme native chief of Fiji given in public assembly before the whole of the tribes from the water sheds of the Rewa river and not for disobedience of my orders. I had on previous occasion recommended Sir Arthur Gordon to remove Tete for disobedience to my orders and those of his chief but His Excellency deemed that it would be a heavy perhaps heavier punishment to him were he impelled to reside with Buli Soloira as a member of his household. . . (CSO/1254/78).

At the end of the disturbance in Colo (September, 1876) whereby the Colo tribes confronted the British Colonial Government for the maintance of their independence and autonomy, 77 Fijian prisoners were on 8 and 9 August, 1876 tried by the Resident Commissioner himself, without the jurisdiction of the Supreme Court. Of this number 20 were sentenced to death, 3 to 5 years, 6 to 3 years, 39 to 2 years, and 4 to 1 year imprisonment with hard labour. Only 4 cases were dismissed, and one prisoner, Nabisiki, was shot dead by the guards while trying to escape during trial. Reporting to the Acting Colonial Secretary of Fiji, the Resident Commissioner wrote:

> . . .Amongst others brought up for trial on this occasion was Nabisiki, a chief of the Nuyakoro tribe, who had a short time previously in a spirit of bravado and defiance visited the camp at Nasaucoko, where he was at once made a prisoner. This man has since the annexation of the colony manifested on all occasions the utmost animosity to the government, although the tribe to which he belonged sent two of their leading chiefs (Taukei Nabuto and Nabiri of Matanibilalevu) as deputies to the meeting held at Navuso by the late Administrator, Mr Layard; and in answer to a direct question put to them had most unreservedly given their adherence, and submission to the British Government.
>
> Nabisiki was the principal "qaqa" or "brave" of this section of the interior of Vitilevu, and had for the past two years exercised a species of direct terrorism over the tribe to which he belonged and was a man of great determination of character, and of undaunted courage and he has undoubtedly

contributed most materially on fortifying the obstinacy of the tribes of this region in their outbreak and persistent defiance of the authorities previous to the suppression of the disturbances now happily at an end.

Such has been the power exercised by Nabisiki even over the minds of his hereditary enemies as the "Kai na Mataku", and also those of Nadi, and Beimana, that some difficulty appeared likely to occur in procuring evidence sufficient to convict him at the trial, and but for the circumstance of his having been seen by the public engaged in attacking the friendly village of Wala and reported in a despatch (Date May 2, 1876). I feel convinced that even the chiefs of that village which he had so secretly laid close siege to for two entire days, would not have dared to give material evidence against him.

During his trial although handcuffed and surrounded by armed guards, he endeavoured to affect his escape at the point where decisive evidence was about to be adduced showing his active leadership in the attack on the before mentioned village, and had succeeded even in reaching the edge of a steep declivity when he was shot dead by the guards.

On the following morning His Excellency the Governor who was present throughout the trials was pleased to commute the sentence of death against twelve of the convicts to five years, and two to ten years imprisonment with hard labour; the six remaining were then executed upon the same day.

So great was the arbitrary power of colonial administrators that life and death were in their hands. Sniders rifles, once used to subjugate the Maoris of New Zealand were also used to quell the disturbances by the club-wielding Colo people. Worse still, coastal Fijians under the command of European officers were used against Fijians of Colo who were trying to maintain their independence. This created more distrust between the two groups and established an unequal relationship whereby the once proud and independent people of the interior developed an inferiority complex relative to the coastal people. The coastal people conversely acquired an attitude of superiority over the people of Colo who were labelled by the colonial administrators of the time as devils or savages. Every effort was exerted to subdue the Colo people and it was once suggested that they should come under the rule of coastal chiefs. Although the Colo chiefs had not legally ceded their land and people to Britain, nor did they sign any contract with the colonial administrators legitimising the British Government's right to subjugate them by force, it was inevitable that the Colo people had to be subdued and subjected to the colonial rule if the whole of Fiji was to be a British possession.

The Fijians of Colo perceived such cession by the coastal chiefs with suspicion fearing that their lands would also be confiscated and that they, the landowners, would be driven to live in certain reserves. There also existed among them a kind of fear of the officers of the government who could either banish them for life or severely penalise them by placing them in servitude for disobeying orders. Being paternalistic and condescending in their administrative approach, colonial administrators continued to sustain this fear and created a sense of no worth and lack of confidence among the people. Lacking self-respect and confidence, the Fijian people as a whole began to belittle themselves and their way of life, and to comply meekly with any orders or directions imposed upon them by colonial officials. They hardly asked questions for fear of being criticised, ostracised or even penalised.

Although the British administrators knew well that the Colo people had not surrendered themselves to colonial rule, they acted as if they had legitimate authority over them. The Colo chiefs were only told of the cession, but had never signed any agreement with the British as the coastal chiefs did.

In a letter dated 4 February, 1876, Governor Gordon reminded Carew that the Colo people were not rebels:

> . . .I don't call the mountaineers "rebels". How can those be rebels who have never submitted? Nor is the police force there for the purpose of forcibly effecting their subjugation. It is in the mountain to protect you and those working to us, but its operation on those against us was and is meant by me to be slow and indirect. (MS 105 A-B. 105B letter of Gordon to Carew. Hocken Library, Dunedin).

Physical force as a tool for submission

It was obvious that many Fijians were vexed at being placed under another group to which they did not belong, and which had no traditional suzerainty over them. The colonial government often ignored the independent and autonomous nature of the many groups. It forcibly brought them together for administrative convenience and often made one of them assume authority over the rest. Some disliked the new *lotu* (religion) and hated being told by another that they must either adopt the new *lotu* or fight. For instance, the Nanuyakoro people were angry because the chief of Navola, by the name of Manumanunivudi, said that the Nanuyakoro people themselves were his and therefore belonging to Nadroga. (Refer to letter of Louis Knolly to Carew from SS Star of South April 29, 1876, Hocken Library).

Nasigatoka village, Nadroga, was another site of judgement for Colo prisoners. Here in the middle of the village is a fenced house site where the prisoners were kept and the trial took place. Some of those who were executed are now buried under the village church. (*Photo—Institute of Pacific Studies, USP*)

Nasaucoko village today. The picture is taken from the top of the hill upon which now runs a road from the Nasigatoka river valley over to the Ba Township. (*Photo—Institute of Pacific Studies, USP*)

The tree of death at Nasaucoko; from the remaining stump of one of its branches indicated by a gentleman of Nasaucoko village, were hanged several people who wanted to maintain their independence from the control of British colonial government. In the background over the other side of the gully is a white cross marking the mass grave of those who were executed publicly for a salutary effect. *(Photo—Institute of Pacific Studies, USP)*

Vatula, an old village fortress, was one of the three sites where the ancestors of some of these young men were judged and publicly executed for bearing arms against the colonial government, defending their autonomy and freedom. The semi-circular arranged boulders on which the young men sit were used as seats during the trial of the Colo prisoners.

This fortress village was on a ridge with very steep slopes on both sides and only accessible by narrow passage ways made of earth mounds across a deep trench at both ends of the village. The fortress overlooks the Sigatoka valley, and it was here that 357 prisoners, were tried and 15 executed. Others including women and children were relocated in villages of the lower Nasigatoka valley such as Vona, Naruku, Tauwau, Nasama, Cuvu, Naidiri, Yadua, Voua, Nasigatoka, Vatukarasa and Vuivuitoa.

This was a means to diffuse their togetherness and strength and to bring the Colo people under control. Some of the descendants of these people are landless today.
(Photo—Institute of Pacific Studies, USP)

Nasaucoko, also known in history as Fort Carnavon, was the colonial government station from which the British Officers and their Native Armed Constabulary units operated against the Colo people who had not submitted to the British rule.

In the foreground is the fortified camp of the British Officers and NAC. Outside the fortification are a number of sentry posts guarding the fortification. Beyond is the fortified village of Nasaucoko.

(Photo—A reproduction by the Fiji National Museum)

Mr Walter Carew, the first Resident Commissioner of Colo (including the provinces of Colo East, Colo North and Colo West). It was greatly through his influence, understanding and sensitivity to the Colo people's way of life, that the Colo tribes were made amenable to early Colonial government rule. He was instrumental in the bringing together to Navuso, in February 1875, 69 chiefs and their retainers to be formally told that Fiji had been ceded to Britain.

(Photo—A reproduction by the Fiji National Museum).

Sir John Thurston, the trusted adviser and confidant of the Fijian chiefs. He defended the Cakobau Government and was against annexation which would erode the power of the Fijian chiefs but enhanced European predominance in Fiji. He was advised by the Commissioners investigating and forcing the issue of annexation not to promulgate the 1873 Constitution which would allow Fijians a greater say in the Legislature. He was threatened of being seized and deported for trial if things went wrong. Under a great deal of pressure and hostility from the Commissioners and other opposition from Europeans, he had little choice but to advise the chiefs to agree to the cession of their country to Britain.

(Photo—A reproduction by the Fiji National Museum)

Governor Sir Arthur Gordon (right) and Captain Knolly (left) ADC to the Governor and one of the Assistant Commissioners among the Colo people. Captain Knolly was in charge of the government forces which brought the defiant Colo tribes under government control in 1876. Both these gentlemen hailed from Scotland.

Captain Knolly and his non-commissioned officers of the Native Armed Constabulary in their official uniforms. Such uniforms were not worn in combat against the Colo people. The *sotia* (soldiers) were normally in traditional attire when on a siege. To the extreme left (standing) was the Sergeant of the Contingent.

(*Photo—A reproduction by the Fiji National Museum*)

Sergeant of the Native Armed Constabulary under Captain Knolly in traditional battle-gear. The top part of the body was bare and decorated with the traditional adornment of a wild boar's tusk.
(Photo—A reproduction by the Fiji National Museum)

British Colonial Administrators, and in particular the Governor, were next to none in Fiji. They were likened to the God on whom life and death depend. The above photograph shows the Governor taking tea on horseback in an interior village of Viti Levu. Social height is equated with physical height. The higher one stands or sits above all others, the higher one's status is. To the Fijian people whatever the Governor said was taken as truth, or *e dina* in Fijian.

(*Photo—Ministry of Information, Suva*)

Nevertheless, through the strong arms of the colonial government, independent and autonomous groups were brought to live and be administered under one authority or chiefdom. Rebellious groups and their chiefs were subdued with strong and harsh measures. Many were tried and condemned to execution or long term imprisonment with hard labour. Threats on their lives and properties by European officers were not uncommon. The arbitrary and despotic power of early colonial administrators and their condescending and arrogant attitudes towards the Fijians who were fighting for their rights is well demonstrated in the following extract from a speech by one of the colonial officers to the chiefs and people of Nuyakoro towns.

To the Chiefs and people of Nuyakoro towns

You the chief and you the people of this town. I will tell you shortly the reason of our coming here. It is on account of the word the governor spoke to you when you gave your *soro* to him. He told you that someday he would send his soldiers to see your towns and his word is fulfilled today. I will tell you something which you will do well to listen to. When this war began you defied the Government and attacked Tatuba and Wala, and when the Ruwailevu people and those at Nabutautau and Naqaqa declared for war you wanted to join them but the Wainimala people came over here and prevented you. This is a fortunate thing for you, if you had fought we should have come here not to talk to you but to take your town, perhaps burn it, and carry you, your wives, your children, and your property away. But you were not able to make war because of the Wainimala people. Remember in the time of the old Government you made war against it— the soldiers came up to your country but you were strong and they were obliged to go back. You thought the Government of this day was the same. No indeed I tell you that the old Government of Fiji is passed, is dead, is buried. Today the Government of England, The Queen of Britain, the Governor, rules Fiji, rules us. Do not deceive yourselves—the Government is strong, the rocks are weak.

There is nothing which the governor cannot do to you if he chooses. You brought your *soro* to him and he accepted it. He said you were to go back to your towns. Think and consider what a great thing it is that you are all here alive in your town. Why? Because he gave you your lives and liberty. He cannot tell you a lie. What he says will come to pass, whether it be good to you or be bad. See what he told those at Ruwailevu, Nabutautau, Naqaqa. Life and death are in his hand alone of men in Fiji. He said to them "Death" and many of them have been killed. He said to you "Life" and you are all alive this day. Do you follow his word. He was sent from England by the Queen to take care of you in this country. He sent his word to you but you did not follow it. Look at Ruwailevu. Look at Nabutautau, Naqaqa. Where are the people today? Death—working—carried away to another part of the country. Are the towns full? You know that the towns are burnt, and that the land is empty. And why? Because they would not follow his word. You alone are alive in your land, so you listen to his voice. He has sent me to you to tell you his word. Listen to me. I came with him from England and I know his mind.

Your are this day in the same position as these soldiers, these officers from Nadi, this chief from Bau, as myself, his children—the children of the Queen of England. He is our father—let us obey him. He loves you and does not hate you. He hates condemning men to die or to work, but he had to do so to the authors of this war that the land might have rest. Hear his law, it is not difficult or heavy, it is easy and light. These things are forbidden. Murder—war—ill-treating women—theft—disputes, troubling the land. The law of the club, of the priests, of the old men is past. The war is over and peace holds the land today.

The Governor says to you stay in your towns—take care of your wives and children, plant as much as you can. Make the land rest, build good houses and clean towns. Let the young men marry and populate the land. Do you live quietly. You old men do not stir up the minds of the young men by reminding them that their fathers have murdered, and therefore they must. Do you help the Governor. If you see a young man going away, stop him. You young men listen to me. Be quiet and look after your wives and property. No one can come here and do hurt to you. If any man does wrong the officers of the government will take him away to be guarded. He will have no rest. They are not going away, they are going to stop in this country to look after you, and if any man does not follow the word of the Governor they will hunt for him every day, week, month, year, and until they find him his land will have no rest. If you want to know anything do not be afraid to go to Nasaucoko. Do not listen to the words you may hear from every place. Listen to the voice of the government officer whom the government approves to stay on this land. He will not tell you a lie.

If I am not there another officer will be in my place. Go to him. Do you bring your food or anything you may want to sell and get property for yourselves. I am glad you obeyed my voice and that the town was full when I came. The Governor hates to see an empty town, and so do I. You have obeyed me and not been afraid, that is good. I will send good news to the Governor and tell him that you stayed in your towns.

We have seen your town and you, and have eaten your present of food and have slept, and now we are going to another town. We have done no ill thing to you. We have not harmed your women or your children or taken a single thing of your property—in old times it was different, a war party would have hurt your women and carried away your property. We are forbidden to do such things. The Governor told me to see that none of these things happened. Do you remember what I have told you and stay quiet and it will be well. If you do not follow my word much evil will happen to you. Whatever the Governor tells you—that follow and your land will have rest. This is my word to you. Do you think over and remember it. I have finished (CSO file 1252/1876).

Fear of the military power and arbitrary authority of the Government rather than respect for what the Government stood for, was inculcated in the minds of the Fijians. Villages had been sacked and burnt to ashes and their inhabitants carried away to servitude, punished, imprisoned, and executed. The Fijian people developed a blind compliance with colonial rule, and for the next ninety and more years, the Fijians hardly questioned rulings by colonial administrators. They were treated as if they were gods and their orders had to be carried out because "life and death were in their hands alone of men in Fiji".

Although Fijians were told that the Governor hated condemning men to die or to work as prisoners, the colonial Government had to do otherwise and found it inevitable to use force and threats on life in order to subdue independent groups of Fijians. Fijians had to be brought under control, and to finally submit themselves to the colonial authorities either for better or worse.

In January 1877, an unstated number of prisoners from Colo, imprisoned in Suva Gaol for two years and less for resisting colonial rule, were shot and killed when they escaped from their work. The following letters from Arthur Gordon and His Excellency Sir A.H. Gordon to Commissioner Carew indicate the rather perturbed feeling, but not too serious concern, about the killing of these Fijian prisoners:

January 3, 1877

My dear Carew,
H.E. (His Excellency) wants to see you at once—All the Kai Colo prisoners working on the road at Suva have escaped! Hush!

Yours Ever,
Arthur Gordon
(MS. 105/A-B MS 105-105B-
Hocken Library Dunedin)

Navosa,
Jan. 5, 1877

My dear Carew,

The official letter which goes with this will show you they have made rather a bad business of it at Suva. I cannot conceive of unarmed escaped prisoners offering such a resistance as should make it necessary to kill them.

If you have made your other arrangement I wish you would go and enquire into this fully—along with Tate and Friend.

Inter alia find out:

a)　where were the guards at the time of escape?
b)　what was the responsibility of the native guard and what of the European N.C.O.?
c)　who gave leave to Ambrose to absent himself.
d)　what orders the police sent in pursuit of the prisoners received?
e)　what was the nature of the resistance met with?
f)　who is Mr W. Clymont and what was his share in the business?

I am much put out about it for killing so many prisoners is a serious matter.

Yours ever,
A.H.G.

Nasova,
Jan. 10. 77.

My dear Carew,
You have I think done excellently well in your arrangements and I trust they may be crowned by success—But I am very sorry about the loss of life. Killing prisoners who one only intended to confine for a couple of years causes me more regret than people being killed in fight or by judicial execution. I suppose however, that it could not be helped.

I shall be glad to see you here again for we have a good deal to consider and decide.

Yours most sincerely,
A.H.G.

Although Sir Arthur Gordon showed a great deal of restraint and remorse about what had happened, he was prepared to go along with the actions taken by his colonial officers if plausible reasons were given to justify the killing of those who disobeyed and escaped colonial authority.

According to the reports sent to the governor, Sir Arthur Gordon, and extracts from the statements and evidence given at the inquiries instituted by the Governor himself, four unarmed prisoners were shot dead when they were trying to get away from their pursuers, the Native Armed Constabulary. In sending the constabulary in pursuit, the Gaoler, Corporal H.D. Wignall of the Royal Engineer Corps, said that he ordered his men to pursue the escaped prisoners and to shoot them if they persisted in running away. But statements given by those who went in pursuit noted that they were to shoot them on sight.

The chief of Lami, Vetaia, who assisted in the pursuit of the prisoners, gave this sworn statement to the stipendiary magistrate doing the investigation: "The Corporal of Engineers called the soldiers and fall them in and armed them and sent them to seek the prisoners and told them to shoot them. The handcuffs were left and guns only taken. He did not tell them to put them in handcuffs or irons but to shoot them". (*CSO* MP. No. 77/11, 77/12/, 77/22). In his report to the Governor, Corporal Wignall also reported that 25 prisoners of the *Kai Colo* tribes were still at large apart from the four who were shot dead near Lami and one who gave himself up and was placed back in custody. (*CSO* MP. No. 77/11). The Resident Commissioner for Colo, Walter Carew, also reported (*CSO* MP. No. 77/22) to the Governor that two of the fugitives had been caught and held prisoner at the Naitasiri gaol. Another prisoner was killed by his pursuers, one of whom cut the prisoner's throat with a hatchet.

Such were the methods by which Fijians were treated and subjugated under colonial rule. For them to comply to the new order and to "respect" or fear their colonial masters, the display of physical power through the use of firearms always had a salutary effect on the once tough-minded and independent Fijians.

The use of arms to subdue a people and to make them surrender their fate to the mightier is as old as Methuselah. Even now the so called Western democracies, at one stage or another in their development, used gun power to either free or protect themselves from the domination of others or to subdue others in order to dominate them. It is paradoxical to observe that to gain and maintain freedom and democracy, a country or people has to ultimately depend upon its fire-power. This is well demonstrated by the nuclear-arms race among the super-powers of the world today; USA, USSR, France, Great Britain and others. Although the use of arms to settle matters and protect one's rights and security is strongly abhorred and repugnant, it is still generally used to either free oneself from the persistent domination of others or to assert one's authority over others. It is still a last resort when peaceful negotiations fail due to greed, craftiness, pride and arrogance, and insensitivity to one's heritage, demands and rights. "We have had an imperial lesson; it may make us an Empire yet", said Rudyard Kipling.

Continuing subjugation of Fijian self-respect

Experiences of early colonial rule developed a kind of fear of Europeans together with an inferiority complex among Fijians which was passed to their descendants. Europeans, and particularly British colonial administrators, had until constitutional independence in 1970, been looked upon by most Fijians with great awe and respect. They were generally perceived to be wise, righteous, and honourable, and always believed to be guardians of Fijian causes and rights in their country. They became so trusted by Fijians that their actions were hardly questioned, and the *turaga ni Bolatagane* (the gentlemen from Great Britain), were more preferable to Fijians as administrators than either Australians or New Zealanders. The British administrative gentleman of the colonial era was an epitome of the relationship between the Fijian people and their chiefs and traditional gods. He was looked upon as the provider for life, protector and liberator, but at the same time he could punish whenever he felt that his authority was challenged. A Fijian group or an individual who insulted the *turaga ni Bolatagane* in one form or another would do well to make atonement or *soro*. For instance the District Commissioner of Colo East, Mr Peck, had the following recorded in his July, 1934, diary:

> Buli Lutu failed to meet me at the boundary of his district, nor was he waiting for me at the first *koro* (Biaugunu village) and I consequently rode straight through without stopping and eventually met him just outside his own *koro* (village). I refused to carry out the *raikoro* (inspection of village) as arranged and rode right through to the last town of the district when I rested the horses and the Buli eventually caught me up there—Heavy *Sorosoro* (offering of large quantity of whale's teeth as atonement) and presentation of *tabua* (whale's teeth), which I eventually accepted and carried out a *raikoro* at that town and arranged to do others on my return—In my opinion, he is one of my best Bulis. (CSO F12/2 Part 4).

As long as Fijians went with the tide and complied with colonial officers' orders and expectations, they would not be harassed but hardly left alone. They had to be acculturated to the new social and political order whereby anything traditional would have to be subservient or abolished. Subtle approaches were often used to deride and discourage traditional values and practices which colonial administrators found irksome or abhorrent to their personal tastes, but had to bear for the sake of acquiring and maintaining their ward's respect and confidence. Not uncommon was the use of direct intervention through the use of restrictive and prohibitive regulations which limited freedom of choice and movement, and discouraged any kind of opposition to the newly established order. Fijians were also made to pay taxes, first in kind and later in cash. They were often forced to leave their villages and families behind and work on contract for cash to pay taxes.

The 1930's quarterly and half-yearly reports of the District Commissioners of the Fijian Province of Colo East conveys some examples of colonial administrative arbitrariness, insensitivity and cultural biases towards their wards. About those Fijians who had been contracted to work on roads and bridges away from homes, the District Commissioner wrote:

> . . . The gang of Fijian labour who had signed on at the beginning of the year under the Masters and Servant Ordinance were not carrying out their work satisfactorily and it was considered advisable to cancel their contracts. Each man was anxious to have his contract terminated. The rationing of these men was proving expensive, and they could not be said to be worthy of their hire. A gang of Indians were recruited as day labourers and they are proving more industrious and more capable of sustained effort ... (D.C's Reports No. 11, 58/30, F12/30 p.4).

On Native Affairs (later Fijian Affairs) and paying of taxes, the District Commissioner reported in his half-yearly report:

> The Fijian is faced with the problem of finding some 2 (two pounds) per annum more or less, for the payment of his Native Tax and Provincial Rate . . . There are some however who even when they have got the money, deliberately waste it, and I have found that a warrant or two served on those who have had the chance to obtain money, actually received it, and either wasted or neglected to pay it, have a salutary effect, the tax either being paid immediately or if the offender is committed to prison. The news spreads and taxpayers realise that though every leniency compatible with

efficiency and practicability is allowed to them, yet they cannot presume on it too much—which I am of the opinion, is the state of affairs suitable to the situation at the present time . . . (DC's Half-Yearly Report F12/ 3 p.1).

On crime, police court records reveal insights on how regulations were used by colonial administrators to effect ultimate control over the Fijian people and influence their values and standard of morality. The District Commissioner of Colo East reported:

Police Court was held on 27 days during the half year. Cases disposed of as follows:

Assault	10
Breach of Pound Order	1
Breach of Prison Regulation	5
Escape from his warrant	1
Found in the dwelling house	1
False information	2
Killing game without licence	4
Larcency	4
Perform native dances without obtaining a licence	4
Retail store licence	1
Riding horse to public danger	5
Tax defaulters	125
Trespass	2
Total	175

In the Provincial courts held in a number of villages under his jurisdiction, the District Commissioner disposed of the following cases:

Adultery	1
Assault	1
Divorce partition	3
Draunikau (Exuvia magic)	1
Fail to carry out orders	9
Living together unmarried	1
Neglect of fire	2
Neglect of communal duties	2
Neglect to provide for family	2
Total	30

Diaries kept by these administrators also reveal their paternalistic and condescending attitudes, which engendered the sense of inferiority among the Fijians. Although Fijian men were not encouraged to leave their villages without permission, they had to go to earn taxes for the Colonial Government. In 1932, the District Commissioner of Colo East recorded on 27 April:

> . . . It was decided that each province would have a quota of men to send each month for the purpose of earning their taxes for 1932. Colo East is to send 100 men per month. By this arrangement it is hoped to have all taxes in by the first week in September (D.C. monthly diaries, F12/2 part 2, 1932.

In April, 1934, entries in the Commissioners' diaries showed the bullying tactics sometimes used:

> Friday 26 . . . Buli Muaira returns from working on new road together with his men, saying that the work is too hard for the pay.

> Saturday 27 . . . Buli Muaira in office he does not wish to go to Wailotua with note for Mr Rix Trott re the work and also to meet S.N.A. ón account of it raining—gave him the option of going at once or resigning his Buliship— he went.

In his official diary for May 1935, the District Commissioner of Colo East entered:

> Wednesday 1st . . . Districts of Waima and Matailobau refuse to go to work on gold fields to earn taxes; this is the second offer which they have turned down.
> Thursday 2nd . . . Soloira people wish to go to Goldfields on Monday and not tomorrow as required. Sent for fifteen men from Nadaravakawalu to work with P.W.D. in Lautoka tomorrow.
> Friday 3rd . . . Only four Nadaravakawalu people wish to go to Lautoka.

There was always an air of immediacy in the demands of these colonial administrators. To refuse or delay resulted in repressive measures. Most administrators did not appreciate much of the Fijian way of life except those aspects which accorded them respect and honour and compliance to their orders as representatives of the colonial executive authority. In his official diary during 1935, on his return from a visit abroad, a particular DC showed insensitivity to Fijian customs:

June 6th . . . Presentation of food by the people of Waima District in honour (?) of my return; these ceremonies are becoming rather expensive to me, as I conceive it to be my duty to show a certain amount of reciprocity.
September 26 . . . Large numbers of Natives gathering at Nakorovatu for Methodist centenary meeting.
Refused permission for the Sergeant and Provincial Constable to take part in *meke* . . . their sense of duty was in my opinion being swamped by their religious (?) fervour.

On March 9th, 1936 the same DC wrote: ". . . The continuous wailing of bereaved natives is getting on my nerves. . ." Such were the attitudes of some of the colonial administrators that even chiefs under their charge developed a sense of complacency and a habit of waiting to be told or directed. The colonial officers became a new highest level of chiefs.

Fear of government officers and what they could do rather than respect for them, kept most Fijians rather quiet and bashful during the colonial era. Disobedience to official or personal demands and orders were usually met with such severe sanctions or repressive measures that those who defaulted would hardly forget. The firmness with which the British colonial administrators dealt with unruly behaviour was something to be reckoned with. Being a proud people in their own land, Fijians had to be subdued by all means available if they were to accept that their new rulers were in control. It was not unusual for a Fijian who assaulted a person of another race, an Indian for instance, to receive fifteen strokes of the whip and three months in gaol. Through such harsh measures, even the leaders of Fijian communities learned to smother their strong feelings against foreigners and to display an outward calmness and apparent indifference when actually within themselves slumbered a whirlwind of heart's emotion. They even developed the polite habit of giving an answer which was thought to please with little regard to truth. Quite often they were taken to the police court for giving false information. Lying to the administration and others thus developed into an art, and tact was a quality they did not lack, enabling them to overcome difficulties and embarrassing situations. They soon learned and knew well their supervisors. Some they would not like to tempt or even persuade because they are persons of one mind. Some others were tried out, for they gave in after a few refusals. They were taught to hide their anger and this often resulted in sullenness. Among themselves, they could easily detect signs and acts of treachery; and among strangers they never felt safe. For almost a century until constitutional independence in 1970, Fijians had become quite "tame" and very amenable to foreign influences and dependent a great deal on their traditional leaders and British administrators to protect their heritage and integrity.

CHAPTER THREE

Indian threat and demand for Political Ascendancy

The 'Indirect' and 'Divide and Rule' policies

From 1874 to the eve of political independence in 1966, British colonial administration kept Fijians separated from other ethnic groups. It controlled change and development with the Fijian social, economic and political structures. Through the Great Council of Chiefs, it received advice and in turn gave direction as to the nature and extent of change and development to be effected among the Fijian people. Much of this was rationalised by colonisers and chiefs alike, under the cachet of safeguarding traditional Fijian culture. This was very acceptable reasoning to the chiefs, whose control and power had already begun to decline at the inception of colonial rule as the result of the introduction of foreign social and political institutions.

Through its administrative policy of Indirect Rule, whereby Fijian traditional leaders administered their own kinsmen according to a number of statutory-supported customary practices, the colonial Government avoided the otherwise inevitable problem of cultural conflict and direct confrontation with any disaffected persons. Until 1970, this policy kept the Fijians at bay and separated them from other ethnic groups. It regulated Fijian village life and controlled direct interaction with other races and their cultures. It also kept the chiefs and their people contented with the colonial administration which they perceived to be maintaining the traditional status quo and only affecting minor disruption and gradual change to their way of life. Obedience to and respect for authority were emphasised. Colonial administrators, during their rounds of Fijian communities, often emphasised the importance of keeping one's own traditions, and particularly those aspects they found convenient to their administrative tasks and the maintenance of their authority and order. In the course of such interaction with the colonial administrators, the Fijian people were often assured that Fijian rights and paramountcy in their own country were safeguarded by the British Crown. There was such trust and confidence in the British colonial rule among Fijians that any suggestion by other races of constitutional independence from Great Britain usually turned into a contentious issue in which Fijian leaders always reaffirmed their loyalty and desire for continuing links with the British Crown. Leading Fijian chiefs were told by their European advisors just before they ceded Fiji to Queen Victoria in 1874, that they must "trust to the Queen's justice and generosity as their sovereign and highest chief to return to them all or whatever part of their gift she may think right, and to govern them righteously and in accordance with native usages and customs". (*Nayacakalou*, 1975, p.83).

Early threats to Fijian dominance

At the time of Cession, the only threat to the maintenance of paramountcy of Fijian interests in Fiji was the presence of European settlers. But European settlers' demands were, under the governorship of Sir Arthur Gordon, carefully contained so that they did not take precedence over Fijian interests. This was evident from Gordon's speech in 1883 when addressing the then Legislative Council on his departure to be Governor of New Zealand:

> . . . that which is at the root of all other dissatisfaction, that which intensifies every grievance and complaint on other subjects . . . is the idea, more or less strongly felt, that the government is not sufficiently active in the promotion and protection of the interests of the white settlers, and regards the native population with too favourable an eye. Now, on this point, it is well that there should be no illusion. It should always be remembered that this emphatically is not a white man's Colony, that the circumstances of its cession and existing facts alike forbid it being so. This is no conquest taken by the sword. This is no empty land just peopled by settlers of our race. The Queen reigns here by virtue of a voluntary cession of their rights to her by the native rulers and owners of these islands—a cession made, among other reasons, expressly for this; that those who ceded might be shielded

from encroachment on the part of settlers which they felt themselves otherwise unable to resist: and it was with full understanding of this, and with a determination to fulfil the obligations it imposed, that the Queen accepted the gift . . . (*Colonial Report*, 1880-83, p. 16).

Fijians feared Indianisation

Through the years of colonial administration, the paramountcy of Fijian interests was gradually eroded through the ambivalent attitude of the Colonial Government which became obliged to look after the interests of other immigrant communities, the most prominent of which were the Indians. First brought to Fiji in 1879 to provide labour for European planters, the large number of Indians in Fiji soon worried the Fijians. For instance by 1900 there were 15,000 Indians in Fiji. This influx caused concern among Fijians, and as early as 1888 the question of their continued introduction was raised in the Great Council of Chiefs by the Native Stipendiary Magistrate of Rewa. The following resolution of the Great Council of Chiefs was passed for the Governor's action:

A large number of coolies have been brought into this Colony, and are still being imported. We notice that many of those who have served their term of indenture locate themselves amongst us: and though we do not wish to be inhospitable, yet we cannot help observing that their number is increasing, and that they are becoming a source of annoyance to us by their thieving propensities and by their customs, which are entirely different from ours and distasteful to us. Furthermore, some of us have been punished when deserters have been found in our villages. We have therefore weighed this matter carefully over in our minds and have unanimously agreed to respectfully ask Your Excellency to explain to us the future position of those who are likely to settle in this Colony. (See *Legislative Council Debate*, 16 July, 1946, p.168).

In his reply, the Governor in 1888 assured the chiefs that the number of coolies settling was not likely to increase rapidly and that it was not clear whether they would settle in any large number. He advised the chiefs, that the Indians who settled in Fiji would be kept under control by the Government and that Fijians should neither allow them to live in their villages nor copy what he termed "their distasteful customs."

Notwithstanding the assurance given by the Governor in 1888, by the end of the indenture system in 1916, there were about 60,000 Indians in Fiji as against 90,000 Fijians. By 1946 Indians numbered about 130,000, and Fijians only 119,000. In the Legislative Council of 19 November 1947, in a speech on the Appropriation Bill, Ratu Sukuna said:

> Fijians fear Indianisation and for this reason: Indians possess an ancient culture of which they are justly proud and from which they have no intention of departing . . . Further, it is because we believe Indian culture to be lacking in the qualities of cooperation, moderation and toleration . . . (*Scarr*, 1983 p. 442).

Indians demanded equality

During the early part of 1920 and again in 1921 there were a number of strikes by Indians demanding increased wages and disrupting communication and services. Led by Manilal Maganlal, an Indian lawyer, Indians pressed for enhanced political rights and social and economic position. Indians displayed their assertiveness and determination to confront Europeans and Fijians in their struggle to obtain political equality in a land to which they had come as immigrants, but where they wanted to establish permanent roots. In order to gain political mileage in Fiji, Indians often held the sugar industry to ransom. They were the main producers and sugar was the main source of colonial revenue. In 1943, during World War II while Fijian men were away at war, another strike by Indian cane farmers took place and the sugar industry was again held as a ransom to their demand for higher cane prices.

On the other hand Europeans dominated both the Executive and Legislative Councils despite the paramountcy of Fijian interests. It was not until 1944 that a Fijian chief, Ratu Sukuna, was made a member of the Executive Council.

In 1929, reacting to a motion by Indian members for common roll, the Colonial Government contended that common franchise was in conflict with its obligations to the Fijian people. However, pressures for the enfranchisement of Indians in Fiji had already begun, and the Colonial Government maintained no wish to defy them. At the same time it pursued no policy to achieve integration or to bring Fijians and Indians into a closer relationship. Social intercourse between the two groups had been spasmodic and discouraged both by Fijian chiefs and Colonial officials. Fijians continued to be administered separately from the Indians and Europeans. They were made to comply with two sets of regulations, the

Native or Fijian regulations and the central Government Laws.

The difficulty of administering three major races with totally different and in important respects contradictory cultural values probably encouraged the colonial rulers to adopt a "divide and rule" policy. It was for them the best way to achieve peace and harmony among the three major ethnic groups with different world views. "Peace in the feud", where loyalty to one's ethnic group was encouraged and at the same time positioned against other groups, become an effective means of strengthening the larger community of the Colony of Fiji and its common loyalty to the British Crown.

The granting of the franchise to Indians and not to Fijians in 1929 was evidence of the colonial government's cautiousness not to make a unitary effort to equalise and bring together the three different ethnic groups. Fijian chiefs also preferred this model. Unfortunately, by being too paternalistic and protective of the Fijian people, colonial officials deprived Fijians of the opportunity to develop political awareness and to achieve their socio-economic aspirations. On the other hand, Indians enjoyed almost free reign to exercise their rights to develop their lot soon after their indenture contracts expired. Although the safeguarding of the Fijian people from the negative effects of foreign acculturation might have been done in good faith, the colonial administration failed to prepare Fijians adequately within the framework of the Fijian Affairs Administration for the difficult task of ultimately living with other races whose presence in the country had been a part of the British colonisation policy.

The Fijian people, however, continued to have confidence in the wisdom of their traditional leaders and colonial administrators in safeguarding the paramountcy of their interests in their own country. While Europeans and Indians were allowed to each elect three of their five representatives to the Legislative Council, Fijians had no direct election but depended on the Great Council of Chiefs to select a panel of names from which the Governor chose five Fijian members, but in practice he merely confirmed the top five on the list. By 1937, equal representation for each of the three major ethnic groups came into being.

As a first step toward self-government, a motion for an unofficial majority was introduced in the Legislative Council in December, 1945. This was not to the liking of the Fijian members, all of whom opposed it. When pressed by an Indian member to adopt a common roll, Ratu Etuate Tuivanuavou Cakobau told the unofficial members that they were displaying racial bias and that he could see no virtue in the rule of numbers, particularly when in a short time, Indians would outnumber Fijians and Europeans added together. Fearing Indian domination, the Fijian members believed in holding onto the official majority with communal representation of a few nominated unofficial members as was then practised. Ratu Tuivanuavou told the meeting that Fijians had every confidence in the Crown; they looked to the Europeans whom Fijians always supported, to think hard and not to give way too easily to democratic ideals—ideals unsuited to a country of three major races who differ in language, culture and religion. These races, he said, would never combine as one people (*Scarr*, 1980, pp. 164-165).

By 1946, Indians surpassed Fijians numerically. Despite their numbers, few Indians enlisted for war services overseas during the Second World War, and others refused unless they received equal pay and conditions of service with Europeans. Fijian loyalty to the British Crown was never questioned; they responded in great numbers to the call to arms and served with distinction in overseas battlefields in Solomon Islands, Papua New Guinea and later in Malaysia.

Fear of Indian domination in a land in which they had been politically dominant was also inherent among Europeans, in particular the businessmen. Universal suffrage, as proposed by Indian members of the Legislative Council, would lead to the political extinction of the Europeans who were over represented in the Legislative Council. The total European electorate of 2,000 enjoyed five representatives, equal to the other major races. On 16 July, 1946, during what came to be known as the Deed of Cession debate, A.A. Ragg, European Member for the Southern Division, moved 'that in view of the great increase in the non-Fijian inhabitants of the Colony, the Council emphasised the covenant entered into through the Deed of Cession, to ensure that the interests of the Fijian race were safeguarded and a guarantee given that Fiji would be preserved as a Fijian country for all time.' (*Scarr*, 1980, p.167). Again on 14 March, 1947, on a motion against the dual system of Government under which Fijians were administered, A.A. Ragg told the Council:

. . . Had Fiji remained a predominantly Fijian country, this system (Fijian system) might through evolutionary process, have led to a reasonable advance of the people. But the . . introduction of an alien race for the exploitation of these islands complicated our system of government and disrupted the perspective of the situation. We who have promised to christianize and develop the Fijians along civilized lines introduced an element into our economy which unless it is controlled, will eliminate both the Fijians and Europeans from the fields of practical politics in this Colony . . . The retarded development of the Fijian race has been largely due to the preoccupation of Government with the commercial exploitation of these islands and the race (Indians) that was introduced for that purpose (*Fiji Legislative Council Debate*, 1947 pp. 108-109).

The Salisbury Despatch as a charter of Indian political rights.

The Europeans' struggle against Indian political dominance, which they were determined never to accept, necessitated Fijian support. This was not difficult to rally, because they shared a common fear of Indian domination. Ever since the arrival of the Indians, Fijians have believed that they, the Indians, would one day return to India. This was partly due to Fijians' inherent dislike of the presence in Fiji of Indians whom they perceived as uncooperative, mean and greedy. They were tolerated on the understanding that most would be returned to India at the end of their indenture. Little did they know that so many Indians were here to stay permanently, rather than as temporary labour migrants for the plantation colonies. In a despatch of 24 March, 1875, to the Provincial Governments of India, Lord Salisbury suggested that those provinces experiencing over-population in particular (such as Bengal), should take an active role in recruiting Indians from the most impoverished section and labouring class to work on European plantations of the British Colonies. The British Government hoped that such deprived people would find the colonies more attractive than the places they came from, and would stay there permanently. This would in turn necessitate the elimination of the return passage to India, an incentive which encouraged Indians to leave for the colonies, and the retention of such labour for the planters.

On the whole, the Government of India rejected Salisbury's proposals and in reply wrote that emigration had little effect on the relief of overpopulation, adding that encouragement of it would be extremely impolitic:

> Our objections have reference to the effect which the direct and active interposition of the Government in this matter would be likely to have on the minds of a people prone to regard with the utmost suspicion the acts and motives of their foreign rulers, and especially on the minds of the uneducated classes from which the immigrants are drawn; and to the difficulty and embarrassment in which the government would become involved by undertaking responsibilities towards the colonies on the one hand, and towards

the emigrants on the other, which it would be practically impossible for it to discharge in a statisfactory manner. (No. 15 of 3 May, 1877, *Government of India*. Reply of Government of India to Lord Salisbury's Public (Emigration) Despatch No. 39 of 24 March, 1875).

On the question of return passage for instance the Madras Board of Revenue stated:

> . . .the withdrawal of the promise of a return passage would be followed by an absolute cessation of the emigration (Page 8 of Item 18 of Lord Salisbury's Despatch quoted above).

Lord Salisbury's Depatch has been quoted by Indian politicians in Fiji, as opposed to the Fijians' Deed of Cession which emphasises the paramountcy of Fijian rights in their country. On this subject the colonial government made a double deal which was not explained to or understood by Fijians until the first Constitutional Conference took place in London in 1965, when the Fijian representatives learnt that the Indians were also full citizens of Fiji, and had been told by the British Government that there was no second class citizen in the British Commonwealth. In this regard it is important to cite Gillion's comments on Salisbury's Despatch as a charter of Indian rights in Fiji.

> ... over the years it has probably unintentionally been taken from its context for it did not refer to Fiji specifically but to all colonies and was a promise that civil disabilities such as the discriminatory pass laws which had been in force in Mauritius and the West Indies would be a thing of the past. Whether it could be stretched to apply to such matters as political representation or land tenure is, to say the least, debatable. Moreover it would appear to have been conditional as an indispensable condition of the proposed arrangements—upon the adoption of the proposal as Salisbury's despatch, did not the Government of India lose the other too? The question whether Indian emigration was to be permanent colonisation or temporary labour migration was left open, and with it the question of Indian rights in the Colonies. Nevertheless, although this paragraph, (On 'Free Men') cannot be accurately cited as a pledge of Indian rights in Fiji, the intention of the British Government was that the Indians who went to the colonies should be allowed to settle permanently and should be treated as full citizens. (*Gillion*, 1962, pp 26-27).

Moreover, when Salisbury made the suggestions, independence for Fiji was probably not considered as a possibility, and therefore Salisbury probably saw no conflict between protecting Fijian land and other rights as promised, and treating Indians equally as British subjects (which would not include access to lands already reserved for Fijians).

It needs to be noted that in 1946, a motion had been put in the Legislative Council by A.A. Ragg to safeguard the Fijian race:

> That in the opinion of this Council the time has arrived in view of the great increase in the non-Fijian inhabitants and its consequential political development—to emphasise the terms of the Deed of Cession to assure that the interests of the Fijian race are safeguarded and guarantee given that Fiji is to be preserved and kept as a Fijian country for all time. (Legislative Council Debate, 1946. p. 163).

After some discussion the motion was amended in order to accommodate the support of other members of the Council. It reads:

> That in the opinion of this Council the Government and the non-Fijian inhabitants of this Colony stand by the terms of the Deed of Cession and shall consider that document as a charter for the Fijian people.

The motion was carried unanimously, with the support of all Indian members. By March, 1947, on the motion on Dual System of the Government in Fiji, and after a long debate on the need to abolish the Fijian Affairs Board regulations which were blamed for Fijian backwardness in social, economic and political development, Mr Vishnu Deo (2nd Indian Member of the Southern Division) further asserted Indian support in safeguarding Fijian interests when he said:

> ...In the matter of the Fijian Affairs Board, Sir, we were in Council and we were a party to the enactment of that ordinance under which that Board was created. At that time, Sir, and even today, I wish to make it quite clear that it was never my intention or the intention of the Indian community settled in this colony to interfere in any way with the Fijian affairs. The attitude of the Indian community in this Colony has always been one of friendly cooperation with the Fijian chiefs and the Fijian people. I wish to make it clear that is our intention for the future as well. We will at all times cooperate with the Fijian chiefs and the Fijian people in all that they wish to do for the welfare of the Fijian race. That Sir, was also clearly enunciated when we had the Deed of Cession debate in this Council in July last year (Legislative Council) Debate, 14 March, 1947 page 112).

Although some Indian leaders publicly declared their support for the Fijian cause, through the years Indians have become economically strong and continued to use their economic strength to enhance their political position in Fiji. As far back as 1933, they demanded common roll which would allow them equal power sharing and decision making in a country where they had come as political non-entities to work on European plantations. Throughout the 1940's and 1950's Indian politicians kept the common roll fire burning and demanded political independence for Fiji. With economic power and numerical size on their side, Indians continued to push for a common roll and all along have aspired to political control of the nation.

With the Fijian community generally protected under the Fijian Affairs Board Regulations, which also restricted direct interaction with other races, it was difficult for the Indians to break through the traditional Fijian communal solidarity, which then existed among the Fijian chiefs and their people: yet this would have to be done if common roll and political independence were to be achieved. Indian demands and aspirations for greater representation and political power have always been perceived by Fijians as an attempt by Indians to dominate Fijians politically and thus take from them the control of their land, which the Indians always demanded be made available, by lease or otherwise, on longer terms and better conditions.

Towards Independence

In the 1950s, Indian and European politicians, and the British Government, kept up the pressure for a review of the Fijian Administration which would ultimately allow Fijians more individual expression, which was restricted under the Fijian regulations which emphasised communalism. This led to two commissions, those of Professor Spate (who reported in April 1959) and Sir Alan Burns (who reported in February, 1960). Although both reports indicated the need to abolish the Fijian Administration, the reports were not acceptable to the Fijian Affairs Board and the Great Council of Chiefs, who agreed only to some modifications. At this time Fijians began to realise that their position in their own country was not as firm as they had thought.

In 1961 Fijian and European members of the Legislative Council did not support the colonial government proposals which would have allowed elected members. A Fijian member said:

We cannot reconcile the implications in these proposals, with the assurances that have been given from time to time that our interest in this our native land shall always remain paramount. (Legislative Council Debates, 1961. p. 185).

In 1962, the Council of Chiefs again voiced its concern on the proposal and felt such a proposal might lead to the relegation of Fijian interests to a position not in keeping with the Deed of Cession. After much careful deliberation, the Council of Chiefs agreed to the election of four Fijian members to the Legislative Council on a communal franchise.

In 1963, the first general election took place, and Fijians tasted their first bitter pill of having leaders selected by political election and on the possibility of non-chiefs being selected. At that time, Fijians generally condemned it improper for non-chiefs to aspire to leadership, though since independence this view has modified considerably. Each of the three main ethnic groups had to elect four of its members to the Legislative Council. The four members from each group then selected two of their number for the Executive Council. Ethnicity or race continued to be the basis for electing and nominating members to the Legislative Council.

Indians hoped that the Fijian chiefs who stood for election would not be voted in to the Legislature, but that Fijian commoners who stood against them would. This was proved wrong: the influence of the chiefs was still so strong that Fijian commoners elected them. The Indian cane farmers supported the candidates of the newly-formed National Federation Party (NFP) which was led by the Indian lawyer-politicians who had led the cane farmers' strike in the 1960s. They were their champions of constitutional change and political enhancement for the Indian community.

In 1964, the Member system was introduced by the colonial government whereby a Fijian, an Indian, and a European elected member held portfolios. The idea of having a Cabinet and the holding of ministerial responsibility was also introduced for the Executive Council members, consisting of elected and official representatives.

Indian demands for constitutional change and political advancement continued nevertheless, and took advantage of the decolonisation movement then in progress. In 1962 the United Kingdom decided to withdraw from its Pacific colonies as soon as possible. Indian politicians continually prodded the United Nations Committee on Colonialism to put pressure on Britain to end its rule in Fiji, to the dismay and unhappiness of the Fijian people and their representatives in the Legislature. Not listening to the Fijian demand for non-interference in the affairs of the country, the United Nations General Assembly pressured Britain to transfer its control of Fiji back to its people.

In 1965, a delegation of Legislative Council members was called to London for a constitutional conference where a deadlock occurred. Fijians asked for the guarantee of the paramountcy of their interests in their own country. The Indians, then a numerical majority and growing, demanded an end to colonial rule and the introduction of a common electoral roll. The Europeans wanted their position secured, and the British delegation stood strong on "no second class citizens" in the British Commonwealth, thus forcing the Fijian representatives to accept equal rights of citizenship for the Indians and other immigrant settlers.

Although the Fijians returned with a constitution which gave them 14 seats in the Legislative Council, two more than the 12 seats for Indians, and four more than 10 for the Europeans and others (General Electors), the majority of Fijians back home were not happy with the constitution which did not return to them the total political power to control their own country.

Indians and Europeans had managed to maintain power-sharing with Fijians and permanently established themselves as citizens of Fiji with exactly the same status as Fijians.

Still being culturally submissive to their own traditional leaders and respectful and loyal to the British Crown, Fijians accepted the constitution with reluctance and disquiet and put their trust in the wisdom of their representatives. On the other hand, Indians were generally unhappy with the constitution because it did not allow them equal or more parliamentary representation in a country in which they were the majority.

In 1966 another election took place and before that, the Alliance Party was formed, based on the Malaysian model. Its major objective was to establish a multiracial political party which would encourage the formation of a truly multi-racial society. A major component of the Alliance Party ever since it started, has been the Fijian Association which was formed in 1956, basically to counter Indian demands for political change. Other associations such as the Suva Rotuma Association, General Electors' Association, All-Fiji Muslim Political Front, came together to form the Alliance Party. It aimed at cross-cultural interaction bringing together the different ethnic groups with their distinct social and political interests, values and aspirations. The NFP, on the other hand, was almost exclusively Indians. It was dominated by Indians in cane farming, business and professions (not by the more numerous Indian labourers, clerks and shop assistants) in the same way that the Alliance was dominated by Fijian chiefs, European business and professional people, and a small proportion of Indian business and professional people. The Alliance Party won the election, due mainly to a division among the Indians, about 15 per cent of whom voted for the Alliance. Hardly any Fijians supported the NFP which was also against the Fijian establishment.

In 1967, the Alliance moved a motion for the introduction of the ministerial system. This caused a stir in Parliament, particularly among the Opposition, which initially did not like the Constitution because it over-represented General Electors (Europeans, Chinese and others) and did not allow for a common franchise. This led to their walk out of Parliament. They did not return to the chamber until after a by-election in August, 1968. Before this by-election the NFP had called for Indian unity or else they would be in danger of losing their security. It continued to denounce the Constitution vehemently, and a by-election resulted in a landslide victory for the Indian dominated party within the Indian communal seats.

The Alliance Party, and particularly Fijians, were very upset about this because they realised that the Indians were determined to acquire power for themselves, and racial tension was high. They denounced Common Roll and political independence which the NFP had been advocating, and strongly reaffirmed their link with the British Crown. At the Navua meeting, some Fijians demanded the attending chiefs to tell them what to do and that they were prepared to fight and die for their *Vanua*. Some of them insisted on the deportation of the NFP leaders and the dismissal of the Indian civil servants who assisted them. Some Fijian leaders even proposed the withdrawal of the Fijian Association from the Alliance Party to form a Fijian Communal Party. Fijians felt that they had been cheated and that Indians could not be trusted even though Fijians had tried to befriend and accommodate them. But with good sense prevailing, Alliance Party leaders made greater efforts to woo Indian supporters. This led to the formation of an Indian Alliance branch of the Alliance Party.

After the 1968 political furore, whereby there was a strong demand by Fijians for Indians to leave the country, Indians took a more conciliatory approach and learned not to push the Fijians politically too far against their wish. The NFP agreed to the Alliance Government proposal for further constitutional discussions in London. Knowing that the NFP was prepared for a compromise, the Alliance Government in November 1969, indicated it was prepared to accept independence. Pleased about this, the NFP agreed to postpone its stand on common roll. It hoped that when the British left, it would be easier for the Indians and Fijians to discuss and decide the electoral system to be adopted.

Thus, with the major difference between the two political parties resolved, independence on 10 October, 1970 was thus agreed to. Two Houses were agreed upon. In the Lower and elected House of Representatives, Fijians and Indians had parity, 22 seats each, (12 communal and 10 cross-voting), and the General Electors 8 seats (3 communal and 5 cross-voting). In the Upper House or Senate, 8 members were nominated by the Council of Chiefs, 7 by the Prime Minister, 6 by the Leader of the Opposition, and 1 by the Council of Rotuma. It was also agreed by both parties that matters affecting Fijian customs and land could not be passed by either House unless supported by 6 of the 8 Council of Chiefs nominees in the Senate. The Senate would act as a chamber for reviewing legislation as well as a protective measure for special Fijian interests.

CHAPTER FOUR

The Last Straw

Cultural insensitivity and misunderstanding

Fijians and Indians were brought together through the strong arms of the Colonial Government, and made to tolerate one another and to learn to live peacefully together in a country which belonged to the Fijians initially. Although these two ethnic groups lived side by side for over a century and sometimes interact spasmodically with each other, it is apparent that their world views are antithetical to one another. The two communities are culturally different in values, beliefs, and aspirations. Through the years they have hardly integrated. Government policies, past and present, continue to keep the two groups apart, in order to avoid inter-ethnic strife.

Fijians are by nature very accommodating and this quality has been enhanced by adopting Christianity which continues to emphasise the principles of love, sharing and care for one another which have always been key principles in traditional Fijian life. In their subsistence way of life, Fijians hardly experienced "poverty" as they were never forced to live frugally or to accumulate food and wealth without redistributing to a wide range of kinsfolk and others. In their lush green bushes and forests, edible roots, leaves and fruits abound. The coastal reefs and mangrove swamps teem with fish, shell-fish, sea-slugs and crustacea such as prawns and crabs. There is plenty to eat and drink, so people have not starved to death as experienced in other countries like India. Moreover, most of the traditional foods are available all year round and were not readily storable. Thus Fijians have not learnt to accumulate for the sake of accumulation or being stingy, but to distribute as everyone else depends upon one another's effort for survival by exploiting wisely their well endowed physical environment. By redistributing the products of their labour, cooperative social and kinship relationships are established and reaffirmed. Thus material wealth and food are expended not only to help others and show care, but also to maintain social togetherness and cooperation in maintaining one's life. To be carefree and well-nourished is the hallmark of a good life.

The Indians, on the other hand, were indentured and became migrants from a generally harsh and severe physical and social environment in which they were highly differentiated, stratified into castes and oppressed by overpopulation and starvation. Fiji was an opportune place to make the best out of it. Although the period of indenture contract was rather dismal, exploitative and tortuous to many, the process of serving or suffering under the indentured system was in fact a baptism of fire which further developed in the Indian personality a great sense of endurance, risk taking and determination. They also had to develop other traits or characteristics which would enable them to survive and become free in a new environment in which they became coolies to the European masters of the plantation economy which had been established in Fiji well before Cession in 1874. Cut off from their extended village and family ties in India, they increasingly become individualistic and egoistic in order to survive and forge ahead economically, politically and socially. Harsh experiences back at home in India, where many foods are both seasonal and storable, compounded by the intolerable and almost slavelike work conditions of the indentured system, had taught the Indians to be frugal, cautious, wise and smart, bordering on being crafty and fraudulent in order to beat off the heat of indenture and the heavy-handed rule of the colonial administrators and plantation owners.

Fijians generally perceive Indians as mean and stingy, crafty and demanding to the extent of being considered greedy, inconsiderate and grasping, uncooperative, egoistic and calculating.

Indians, on the other hand, view Fijians as "jungalis" or bushwhackers, still behind the times and backward, naive and foolish, and generally poor. They are seen as lazy, proud and extravagant, pound-foolish and undependable.

These perceptions of each other are nearly always subdued and latent yet only need some slight provocations to bring them to the fore, which at times culminates in open physical confrontations. Fortunately the strong arms of the Government usually fall heavily upon the offenders so that superficial racial harmony is maintained at all costs. Throughout the colonial period the two major communities lived side by side in a seemingly cordial co-existence, but hardly any real or deep-rooted harmony. Tolerance of one another has been the key principle all along. Such tolerance can be forced by a colonial power but can only last in an independent nation if each community understands the other's culture and is sensitive and respectful of the other people's beliefs, values and aspirations. But increasing economic prosperity among Indians and their enhanced political position in Fiji caused them to become more desirous and ambitious to acquire ultimate political control and leadership in the country. From the 1960s to the 1980s, they tried to do this alone, but from the mid-1980s, they came to realize that they could only wield the power from behind a facade of Fijian leadership. In attempting to do this, Indians have trodden on very sacred ground and have been very insensitive and indifferent to Fijian feelings and to Fijian aspirations to again become masters of their country. Fijians had long feared that Indians would one day rule Fiji, the country of their heritage and for which their ancestors had shed their blood and sweat, and lost lives defending it. It is ironic that Fijians had forcibly given the country away to the British Queen, Victoria, in order to protect its people and land from the encroachments of others who were intent at grabbing and owning it.

Taukei and Vulagi Concepts.

Well before the Europeans and other foreigners arrived in Fiji and up till now, Fijians have always categorised the population or inhabitants of the country, or of any locality or village, into two main divisions. A person is either a *taukei* (indigenous or owner) or *vulagi* (visitor or foreigner) in any place.

The *taukei* are the indigenous or the original or first to be in a locality or those who conquered them in war. They thus claim rights of ownership and control over the land. Any others who arrive later to settle with the original settlers (or subsequent conquerers) of that area are known as *vulagi*: visitors, or foreigners. For instance, the original founders of a village are the *taukei* or owners of that village, and they would defend it from all other claimants who were not the descendants of the first inhabitants or founders of the village. The first to garden in an area becomes the *taukei* of that piece of land and he will defend it from all others. It was on these traditional criteria that the various Native Land Commissions of the British Colonial Government investigated, decided and established rights of ownership to Fijian land.

Through the good will of the *taukei*, however, subsequent arrivals can be accommodated and assigned house and gardening sites. They are only allowed the rights to use those designated areas but not the rights of ownership which only belong to the *taukei*, or their direct descendants.

The *taukei* are normally at the forefront of the discussion in decision making. The vulagi are allowed to participate in the process but they must not be seen domineering or forceful. Usually when a *vulagi* behaves in this way, he is then reminded of his position as *vulagi* by the *taukei*, who quite often points the way out for them to disappear.

A Fijian, either man or woman, who marries into another *vanua* (tribe and locality) and produces children in that area and has lived and toiled with the members of the *vanua* for long cannot for an instant claim or aspire to a decision making position which only *taukei* are entitled to. He should never claim or pretend that he is a *taukei*.

Traditional protocol requires the *vulagi* to be humble and know well his role and position in the context in which he or his ancestors have not been original settlers or *taukei*. His descendants will have little claim either, and they will continue to be *vulagi* unless they go back to where they originated, or unless their mother was *taukei*, in which case the *mataqali* (kin group) can accept them as members if it so decides. As long as they work hard for the community or vanua in which they are settled and accommodated, the *vulagi* are by definition part and members of the *vanua* in which they live.

The *vulagi* are generally the work-horses of the physical and social settings in which they are established. They generally provide their best in order to be acceptable to the *taukei*. It is prudent, however, not to boast or publicly claim honour for their contributions in support of the *taukei* cause, for such contributions and support are expected elements of cooperation if the *vulagi* are to be acceptable and accommodated into the *taukei* community. It is for the *taukei* to give recognition to the *vulagi* for the contributions and cooperation rendered. *Vulagi* must never use their effectiveness in supporting the *taukei* cause to publicly belittle the *taukei*, or to demand more. Any such personal affront deeply offends a *taukei*, and is not easily forgotten. A sarcastic remark, or to taunt his inability, makes him unhappy and he will either give you proof to the contrary, or resolve quietly to bide his time for revenge. If the *vulagi* continues to be boastful, arrogant or to demean the *taukei* for their ineffectiveness, no amount of support or gifts will make the *taukei* happy: they will simply show the *vulagi* the direction to get out fast. All is well if the vulagi is humble, respectful, tolerant and cooperative. He respects and recognises the *taukei* for what he is and not only for what he can do for the *vulagi* himself.

The *taukei* on the other hand has certain obligations to the *vulagi*. The *vulagi* is usually welcomed and accommodated, loved and cared for. He is protected and allowed access to the natural resources for his sustenance and that of his family. As long as the *vulagi* uses the resources for the support of his family and for the cause of *taukei ni vanua*, (owners of the land), he is free to do as much as he can. Even when conquered, the subdued provides tribute and is generally free to do as he likes as long as he does not abuse traditional protocol and expectations. To go beyond that for personal gain and recognition is to invite harassment and some kinds of sanction which either send the vulagi away or make his life more difficult if he insists on staying. The only way out from this impasse is for the *vulagi* to *soro* or make atonement to the *taukei* by ritually offering him traditional wealth and gifts, and publicly pronouncing his weaknesses and the wish to be pardoned and again accepted. The *taukei* is in turn expected to respect and accept the *vulagi's* effort at reconciliation as long as it is genuine.

The best analogy to this *taukei* and *vulagi* relationship is that of the host and guest. The host is the *taukei* and the guest is the *vulagi*. Each must play fair and be honest with each other and understand well each one's obligations to the other. The host is generally in command, and the guest must comply with the host's requirements if he is to be accepted and accommodated. If the guest does not comply to the host's expectations then he may very well leave before he is thrown out of the house.

Democracy and equality, a guise to political dominance

This "host and guest" relationship continues to be challenged and upset by the introduction of the human rights concept in which all are considered equal. The British Colonial Government also introduced a parliamentary democracy unsuited to the Fiji context in which Fijians still strongly claim their special position as the autochthonous people because they belonged here first, well before anyone else settled here. And very few of the immigrants came at Fijian invitation or with Fijian acceptance. Their chiefly ancestors ceded Fiji to Great Britain explicitly to be protected from the encroachments of others. Fijians felt cheated when, at Independence, these others were given equal rights of citizenship and thus political standing in a country in which the Fijians believed they should have the predominant control. This is not something they have decided only *since* their ancestors ceded Fiji to Queen Victoria, but it was a part of the Deed of Cession which colonial administrators so often emphasised when questioned of the status they afforded the Fijians. For example, Governor Jakeway said in 1965, in reply to a question from an Indian representative of a Nadi newspaper, Mr R.K. Sharma, that it was inconceivable that Britain would ever permit the Fijian people to be placed politically under the heel of an immigrant community. Sir Derek was only stating what he thought was a fact and he had not realised that would cause offence among the Indians in Fiji:

> What I am trying to say is not new, surely. I thought it was common ground that the Fijian people—the autochthonous people—have a special position in Fiji because they belonged here first, long before anyone else came here. I am sorry if I seemed offensive to anybody, but it is a fact. It is indeed part of the Deed of Cession. (*Fiji Times*, 2 March, 1965)

When asked if he feared racial troubles in Fiji as had occurred in other parts of the world, he mentioned two reassurances that had to be given. One was to reassure the Fijian community that it would not be dominated in what it regarded as its own country. The other was to ensure that the Indian community was given security of occupation of land so that it could continue to derive its livelihood from the land.

It was evident all along that most Indians in Fiji did not want to accept and respect the special position of Fijians in Fiji. Their excessive and frequent demands for political "equality" and their constant drive to achieve political leadership in Fiji displayed their arrogance, lack of respect and insensitivity to the rights of indigenous Fijians to once again hold political paramountcy in their country. They overemphasised and overreacted to the concepts of political equality and democracy in a bid to discourage the Fijian demand for political priority in his country. Democracy and equality have since been the catchwords of the Indian political struggle to discourage and out-manoeuvre Fijian political efforts and aspirations. Using their demographic and economic dominance, Indians continued to emphasise the need for a more democratic process of elections by the adoption of a common roll voting system of one man one vote. In this way Indians hoped to achieve political control in Fiji.

Through the 1970 system of election to Parliament, Indians had twice almost controlled the country. The 1970 election system required a person to vote four times. Apart from voting on communal roll, all voters were also required to vote on national roll, whereby they had to cross vote for 10 Indian members, 10 Fijian members, and 5 from others who were neither Fijians nor Indians. The national cross voting was intended to make each ethnic group listen to the other and to share power. In two elections, the Indian-dominated National Federation Party and Coalition Party (NFP and Labour Party) toppled the Alliance Party in 1977 and 1987 respectively. Indians, Fijians and others who stood for the multiracial Alliance Party of Ratu Mara had little chance to win seats in electorates where there were more Indians. Although cross voting continues to be frequently expanded by Indians as a way towards political integration, Fijians see it as a means towards Indian control. That national cross voting is a way towards political integration is too simplistic a view and is insensitive to the deep feelings and existing aggression among Fijians in relation to Indian political aspirations.

But Fijians were not naive. They knew the motives behind Indian suggestions for a common roll voting system and rejected the concept of one person one vote but agreed to try out cross voting and found it unpalatable too. Quietly Fijians bided their time and waited for an opportunity to reassert their rightful position once and for all.

Fijian experiences with the colonial rule did not show them any rule based on democracy. All that they knew was the presence of an authoritarian colonial power on which life and death for the Fijians depended. During the later period of colonial administration, a much more benevolent dictatorship with some token adherence to democracy as it is known in Western Europe was experienced. Britain never practised democracy in Fiji and only recommended others to practise it after Britain left. But one thing the Fijian is convinced of is that his Fijian system of organising and doing things is more democratic than all the political manipulation and lobbying he has come to experience during the so-called democratic process of election to parliament of later years, in which money, advertising, demagoguery and media manipulation play such a part.

For the Indians to talk about democracy and equality greatly irritated the Fijians who were always reminded of Indian non-cooperation and minimal involvement in the struggle for the maintenance of democracy during World War II. While Fijians gave their lives to fight for the maintenance of democratic rule in the world, Fiji Indians were not interested in the fight for democracy but in their own individual enhancement, demanding more pay and special protection of their properties and families. Due in part to their non-cooperation during such difficult times, Indians could not acquire the trust and acceptance of the Fijians as good neighbours and countrymen. Today Indians talk about Fiji as their country, but to the Fijians, this is not so, because they refused to sacrifice their lives for its defence when the threat of Japanese invasion was real and close. Money and the accumulation of individual wealth and property are more important to them than defending the country which they now proudly claim as theirs too.

On the other hand, Fijians have always supported the fight for freedom and democracy. From 1914 to 1918 they sent troops to Europe to repel German expansion, and from 1939 to 1945, they participated fully in the war to stop German and Japanese conquest and dictatorship. From 1951 to 1956, they again sacrificed their lives for the maintenance of freedom and democracy against communist insurgence in Malaya. In all these struggles for democracy and freedom, the Indians as individuals and as a community hardly involved themselves but continued to benefit from the toil, sweat and loss of lives of the Fijians in an effort to maintain political stability in the world.

Fijian peace keeping forces have now been in the United Nations Force in Lebanon and in the Multi-National Force in Sinai for several years, and contributed forces to the tasks of bringing freedom to colonized people in Zimbabwe and Namibia. Fijians have always offered their services to defend peace and freedom. In such efforts, only a very small number of Indians were involved.

Fijians are peace loving and this quality has made it possible for other races to live with them for more than a century without any bloody conflict, even though there was little democratic rule of the kind now propounded by the Indians. The lack of true commitment of the Indian community to Fiji is evident and well known to Fijians. They have been perceived to be always on the move and generally off to greener pastures whenever better and more profitable opportunities offer. They do not choose to return to India, but go instead to Australia, Canada, USA and New Zealand. They have been noted for their tactics of withdrawing their economic, social and political support in order to wreck the country's economy and its social services if their wishes and demands are not met. They are interested in gaining power for themselves which will in turn give them the security of their position and property in Fiji.

Although Fijian leadership was conscious of the danger of Fijians losing power, it had hoped that Indians would cooperate in an effort to establish

Freedom and democracy for Fiji had been and has continued to be earned through toil and sweat, and the sacrificing of Fijian lives at home and in overseas battlefields. In the above photograph the Governor was inspecting the 1st Battalion, Fiji Infantry Regiment, prior to their departure for the Solomon Islands campaign against Japanese invaders during World War II.

(Photo—Ministry of Information, Suva)

Fighting for freedom and democracy in the world, and for their chiefs and country, the Fijian 1st Battalion, Fiji Infantry Regiment, marched through Suva, on their way to the wharf to board the "President Hayes" for active service overseas on 13 April, 1943. At the wharf it was difficult for the soldiers to embark the ship as relatives and friends hugged their loved ones and wailed for the departed brave sons of Fiji.

Fighting for freedom and democracy, and for their chiefs and country, the 3rd Battalion, Fiji Infantry Regiment, on 12 March, 1944, were transported in U.S. Army trucks to the Suva Wharf to board the "Poleau Laut" and to join their Fijian brothers in the 1st Commando and 1st Battalion overseas. They had to be taken in trucks to avoid the harassment and difficulties of farewelling those who were going to fields of death experienced during the 1st Battalion embarkation for overseas assignment.

Photo—Ministry of Information, Suva)

Members of the 3rd Battalion, Fiji Infantry Regiment on their way to Suva Wharf for their military assignment in the Solomon Islands during World War II.
(Photo—Ministry of Information, Suva)

Fijian soldiers in a march past in Batu Pahat, Malaya. Leading the contingent was the Commander of the 1st Battalion, Fiji Military Forces, stationed in Malaya, Lt. Colonel Ratu Penaia Ganilau. (Now the President of The Republic of Fiji). Well known as the "best jungle fighters in the world", a recognition gained from the Solomon Islands campaign during World War II. Fijian soldiers were again required by the British Government to assist in the containment and elimination of communist insurgents in the jungles of Malaya.

(Photo—Courtesy of the Fiji Military Forces)

A patrol of Fijian soldiers going into action against communist terrorists in the Malayan jungle. They again reaffirmed their reputation as the best jungle fighters when they finally wiped out communist terrorists in the dense and humid tropical rainforests of Malaya.
(Photo—Courtesy of the Fiji Military Forces)

Through flooded creeks, marsh lands and thick bushes where blood-sucking leeches and mosquitoes lurk in abundance, Fijian soldiers toiled sweated, and lost lives in the fight against communism and dictatorship.

In the United Nation peace keeping forces in Lebanon, Fijian soldiers again displayed a high standard of discipline and courage in guarding their outposts. Peace keeping duties in Lebanon, and lately in Sinai have had a salutary effect on these feared jungle fighters, that when the coup d'etat happened in 1987 they handled it with a high standard of discipline and efficiency with no loss of life.

a truly multiracial society in Fiji. This call for multiracialism by Fijian leadership was rejected by the vast majority of Indians. They did not vote with the Fijians but continued to support the candidates endorsed by their Indian leaders. Always, it seemed, the promises of support from the Indians were there, but when the election results were counted, it was a different story. The majority of Indians voted for the candidates of their own ethnic party (NFP) who were dedicated to winning the elections and forming the government. This was a slap in the face of Fijian leadership, and confirmed the suspicion of most Fijians that Indians were out to grab power. The situation became almost intolerable for many Fijians.

Indians continued to demand more and became garrulous about their economic strength and contributions to the development of the country which they also claimed as theirs. They repeatedly announced and tried to portray the importance of their presence in Fiji and did everything they could to show their indispensability in the country which had nurtured and nourished them through the goodwill and favourable consideration of the indigenous Fijians. If it had not been for such goodwill and the accommodating nature of the Fijians as a whole, the Indians would not have achieved what they have achieved today. Fijians allowed their land to be leased to Indians for thirty years at a time. Even this did not satisfy the Indians who still wanted much longer periods and better conditions.

Fijian trust and generosity was shown in 1940, with the formation of the Native Land Trust Board. With the persuasion and encouragement of their chiefs, the Fijians agreed to relinquish direct control of their tribal lands so that secure agricultural leases could be issued to Indian farmers. In this way some of the most fertile areas of Fiji became a source of rural wealth for many thousands of Indians with legal tenancy at only six percent of the conservatively assessed capital value, which is far below the market value for such land.

In fact, Fijian chiefs and other elements of the Fijian hierarchy helped create and preserve political stability which provided the very foundation for the emergence of the flourishing and prosperous Indian business and farming community.

Multiracialism and mockery of Fijian paramountcy

During the 17 years of Alliance Government rule from independence in 1970 to the election of April 1987, it made several efforts to accommodate Indian demands for Fijian land and other aspirations, and tried to build a government of national unity among the multiracial people of Fiji. In an effort to establish a truly multiracial society the Alliance Government was perceived by most Fijians to be increasingly accommodating to Indian demands and neglecting Fijian interests in what Fijians themselves firmly believe to be their rightful heritage. This gave rise to the formation of the Fijian Nationalist Party led by Sakeasi Butadroka whose political slogan of "Fiji for the Fijians" often irked and embarrassed the Alliance Government. During the Parliamentary Session of 9 October, 1975, Butadroka moved a motion for the repatriation of Indians back to India:

> That this House agrees that the time has arrived when Indians or people of Indian origin in this country be repatriated back to India and that their travelling expenses back home and compensation for their properties in this country be met by the British Government, (*L.C.D.* Oct., 1975. p.1104).

After a prolonged discussion on the motion Ratu David Toganivalu, one of the Fijian leaders in Council who was greatly respected by the Indian community, affirmed the validity of this anti-Indian feeling among Fijians by stating:

> . . . Ethnic feeling and rivalry is very real. It is always skin deep at the best of times, and when it is aroused, it does not take long to come to the fore. One must be very honest, Mr Speaker, in saying that all Fijians consciously, but mainly unconsciously, feel at times in terms of what is expressed in the terms of the motion. There is no use hiding about it . . . I have got to say this, Mr. Speaker, because if you have got to vomit, vomit properly, right onto the floor, and examine why certain members of our community are vomiting (*Parliamentary Debates*, 1975, p. 1203).

To stop the uttering of political remarks with racial overtones, which would not assist its effort at enhancing multiracialism in Fiji, the Alliance Government in 1976 enacted a law forbidding comments of a negative racial character (Public Order Act No. 20 of 1976). Under this law the leader of the Fijian Nationalist Party, Sakeasi Butadroka, was found guilty and gaoled in 1977 for six months, thus rendering him incapable of winning the next election for parliament.

The Fijian Nationalist Party, although not openly supported by many Fijians who still accepted or respected Fijian chiefly leadership in the Alliance Government, has since its formation been publicly displaying the private and quiet feelings of most Fijians. They have never been happy with the 1970 Constitution which provides equal power-sharing with Indians and the possibility of Indian domination. In speaking against the Amendment of the Public Order Bill in Parliament on 13 August, 1976; Sakeasi Butadroka said:

> Why are the Fijians, Sir, now speaking and starting to voice what they think are their rights and privileges in this country? I think it is timely, Sir. They should cry out now after the constitution talks in London in 1970. This happened in other countries—just give them time . . . But here in Fiji, Sir, and I repeat this, the indigenous race and owners of this country are now beginning to raise questions about what the leaders, especially Fijian leaders, did in the 1970 Constitutional talks (*Parliamentary Debate of the House of Representatives*, 1976, Part II, page 689).

In two elections (1977 and 1987) the Alliance Party was defeated, not only because Indians voted en bloc for the National Federation Party, but because Fijian support for the Alliance Party was no longer intact. Disillusionment and dissatisfaction with the Alliance Party Government policy on the leasing and development of Fijian land for public purposes and for Indian economic enterprises was prevalent among Fijian landowners. Alleged and perceived corruption and nepotism within the Alliance Government was enough to make the disaffected Fijians switch their support and give their votes to another party which would deliver the goods. But even in 1987 only 9 percent of Fijians voted for the NFP/Labour Coalition, fewer than the number of Indians voting for the Alliance.

Election campaign promises to rural Fijian villages by Alliance Government Ministers did not materialise, nor were the reasons for their non-execution explained to the electorates. Suspicion and rumours of collusion among Alliance Party leadership with prosperous businessmen were rife. Many Fijians increasingly felt that their loyalty and trust in the Alliance Government leadership had come to little but increasing material wealth for the powerful and the few who associated with them.

Increasing individualism among Fijians was another factor which undermined Fijian support for the Alliance Party. The past effort of containing Fijian togetherness and control through the then Native or Fijian Regulations which emphasised communalism had been relaxed by the revocation of these regulations in 1966. Since then, Fijians have been allowed a great deal of choice which adversely affected traditional Fijian communal solidarity. Although legally allowed to choose, Fijians are still culturally expected to live communally in villages and to continue to comply with traditional authority and expectations. From 1963 to the 1980s, it has been apparent that those in Fijian leadership and authority sensed that they had lost the unequivocal support, the uncompromising compliance and the wide respect they had enjoyed during the colonial period. Most Fijians have taken the opportunity of being freed from the yoke of subservience to traditional authority and obeisance then supported by statutory sanctions. They have asserted their individual rights and freedom and made new social links and political alignments. This has posed a threat to the long-established Fijian traditional order and its hierarchical structure of chiefly authority.

Where chiefs have become unchiefly by no longer adhering to their traditional roles of serving and protecting their people, but involved themselves more in the market economy, accumulating material wealth and cash without distributing this to their village folks, there is a tendency for such chiefs to command little respect from the people, though they may at times be reluctantly listened to or respected. In some instances chiefly position and power have been openly challenged, particularly by those who felt deceived and frustrated by those with such power. The increasing interest and active participation of Fijians in modern socio-economic and political systems with different power bases have also undermined the effectiveness of traditional Fijian leadership focusing on the chief. Thus, traditional Fijian leaders have for some time felt they are losing control of their followers. Laxity and too great a freedom among Fijians are blamed.

Fijian dilemma

Fijians have long been in a dilemma. Continually advised by their leaders of the importance of maintaining their customs and traditions which insist on communalism, at the same time they have been urged to be involved in commercial enterprises which emphasise individualism, and also to accept the policy of multiracialism which the Alliance Government of Ratu Kamisese Mara advocated between 1970 and 1987. Although the Alliance Government policy of encouraging multiracialism and commercial individualism among Fijians and other races living in Fiji is important, it must not be carried to the extent of challenging Fijian paramountcy and Fijian leadership.

Apart from the public political stand of the Fijian Nationalist Party, 'Fiji for the Fijians', Fijians in general have been waiting quietly for an opportune time to assert their demand for political control of their country which was shared equally with Indians through the 1970 constitution. This paved the way for Indian control of Fiji. Apart from the quiet dissatisfaction among Fijians with this equal-power sharing, economic disparities between Fijians and Indians have obviously worsened, with Fijians lagging far behind. In commercial activities, they have become consumers, with few management roles. In government services and statutory bodies, Indians outnumbered Fijians and other ethnic groups, except in the Fiji Military Forces.

An estimate of ethnic ownership of business enterprises supplied by the Office of the Registrar of Companies June, 1987 shows that 50% are for Indians, 15% for Fijians, 20% for others, 15% joint venture. This represents all the 7000 businesses registered, including limited liabilities companies and small family owned businesses. The joint ventures included all of the above ethnic groups.

According to the Director of Public Prosecutions, there were 12 Fijian lawyers as against 197 Indian lawyers, and 1 Fijian as against 10 Indian judges (including Indian expatriates) before the coup in April 1987.

In the table below, the ethnic distribution of jobs in the Public Service is shown and Indians again predominate over Fijians and others.

Public Service Staff-in-Post to 14 May, 1987

Occupational Classification	Fijians	Indians	Others including expatr'tes
Generalist and Specialist Admin.	1,176 (41%)	1,506 (55%)	117 (4%)
Construction Services	154 (48%)	125 (38%)	45 (14%)
Medical Officers	88 (29%)	175 (57%)	42 (14%)
Dental Officers	62 (38%)	97 (60%)	4 (2%)
Para-medical Officers	96 (33%)	180 (63%)	12 (4%)
Pharmacy Officers	13 (32%)	27 (68%)	-
Mechanical and Electrical Eng.	49 (40%)	59 (48%)	15 (12%)
Police Officers	831 (52%)	732 (45%)	43 (3%)
Radio & Electrical Engineering	278(42%)	320 (48%)	65 (10%)
Procurement and Supply Officers	57 (34%)	110 (65%)	1 (.59%)
Teaching	2903 (44%)	3534 (54%)	155 (2%)
Upper Salary	62 (35%)	74 (42%)	40 (23%)
Legal Officers	3 (19%)	8 (50%)	5 (31%)
Judges	1 (14%)	2 (29%)	4 (57%)

(Source: Fiji Public Service Commission Report, 1987)

In relation to ownership of land, Fijians hold 83% of the area of land in Fiji, although much of it is of rugged hilly nature with steep slopes. It has been suggested that it is worth only 20% of the total value of all the good arable land owned by Indians and Europeans and others. Indians now hold 80% of the arable freehold land, 96% of Crown agricultural leases and about 80% of leases of Fijian land.

The opportunity to wrest power away from the Indians had been suppressed by the predominance and strength of Fijian chiefly leadership in the Alliance Government. The defeat of the Alliance Government in the 1977 election by the National Federation Party, almost provided such an opportunity but it was obviated by the then Governor General, Ratu Sir Joji Kadavulevu Cakobau, who summarily called back the defeated Alliance leader, Ratu Sir Kamisese Mara to form a Government, when the NFP took several days to argue over who should be their Prime Minister.

A civil war was close at hand. Fijian representatives were sent from the islands of Kadavu, Yasawa and elsewhere in Fiji to inform the Governor General, Ratu Sir Joji Cakobau, that men were ready to be called to action to regain control of their country. It was again the chiefs who discouraged what could have been a catastrophic attack on Indians.

Power changing hands

It was obvious all along to some political and social observers, both locals and outsiders, that as long as Fijian traditional leadership predominated in running the Government, possible physical confrontations with Indians would be kept under control. The defeat of the Alliance Party in the 1987 election thus brought out openly the long suppressed wish of the Fijians to be assured of their priority in the rule of Fiji.

Although Fijians were appointed as Cabinet Ministers and a Fijian was made Prime Minister in the Labour/NFP Coalition Government, which defeated the Alliance Government, most Fijians believe that Indian politicians had used Fijians only as a front in their struggle for power. A small Fijian minority (about 9%) including some disaffected educated Fijians who were not happy with the arbitrary use of the power by the Alliance Government, and some who had aspired to political roles in the Alliance but fallen out of favour and some Fijian urban dwellers and rural villagers whom they persuaded and impressed with the weaknesses of the Alliance rule, voted for the Labour/NFP Coalition. More Indians than Fijians were thus voted into Parliament (19 to 7). In fact there were more NFP candidates voted into Parliament (17) than those of the Labour Party (11). As Robert Keith-Reid noted:

> . . .the new Government isn't much a Labour Government, but mostly a National Federation Party. Honestly, how many seats would have Labour won without NFP help? The Coalition picked up only 9.46% of the Fijian vote, 16.18% of General vote but 82% Indian vote . . .
> . . . As a democracy in which the will of the minority is being imposed on the majority, let's wish the Bavadra Government, and all of ourselves, a lot of luck anyway. After all, who really wants our national apple cart spilled? Unfortunately it is a cart that can be easily pushed over if the driver isn't careful . . . (*Fiji Times*, 18 April, 1987 p.7)

Although Labour Parliamentarians were in the minority it was in the interest of the Coalition government to appoint six Fijians as Cabinet Ministers. Even so there was an Indian majority in the Cabinet. For the same reason, to keep the Fijian public somewhat pacified, the Fijian leader of the Labour Party, Timoci Bavadra, was made the Prime Minister. The NFP had gone out of its way to be accepted by the Labour Party to form a coalition, as the only way to defeat the Alliance Party and take over the reins of the Government which it had been trying to hold for over 20 years.

The Coalition's main objective for the 1987 General election was to topple the Alliance Government, but without due consideration or sensitivity to the consequences of power changing hands—from a Fijian-dominated to an Indian-dominated government. Thus Bavadra and his 9% of Fijian supporters have been generally seen by other Fijians as pawns in the inter-racial struggle for political power who have been used as a tool for achieving the Indian political aspiration to ultimately control Fiji.

It was unfortunate that Bavadra had not sensed this feeling when he accepted the NFP's offer of a coalition. His Labour party could have won a number of seats in Parliament alone and then acted as a power broker controlling the Alliance Party and the National Federation Party, both of which were polarised along ethnic lines. The Labour Party too was overwhelmingly non-Fijian in number, finance, organisation and influence. In ignoring Fijian feeling and succumbing to the tempting offer of the National Federation Party, Bavadra's Labour Party was no longer independent or immune from the anti-Indian feeling that existed among many Fijians but which was suppressed and contained during the years of colonial Government and 17 years of Alliance Party rule. Even as late as January, 1987, this anti-Indian feeling was again publicly expressed by the leader of the Fijian Nationalist Party, whose views were widely but quietly supported by many Fijians.

> Butadroka advocates thinning out of Indians in Fiji, "Either they stay here and we go down or they leave. There is no alternative. After 16 years, Fijians have lost out in the Civil Service, in employment, in education—what will happen to us in another 16 years". (*Fiji Times* 1 January, 1987, page 7).

On the eve of the coup d'etat

Suspicion of the Bavadra Government increased when Bavadra offered a number of top Government posts to its political supporters and made Mr Jai Ram Reddy Minister of Justice, even though he was not an elected Member of Parliament. Its action was thus being closely watched, in particular by Fijians who had for some time been irritated and provoked by arrogant and insensitive statements made by Indians through the media, emphasising their political achievements and economic contributions to Fiji and ignoring the presence, feelings and contributions of Fijians. Indians had also been over-playing the idea of equality in a country in which they were increasingly dominating both the civil service and commercial sector.

The first open display of the dislike of the Labour/National Federation Coalition Government was staged by groups of Fijian villagers in the Ba area. Tavua villagers on 19 April, 1987, put up three road-blocks on public roads saying they disapproved of the change of government. In a protest march through Tavua town, about 150 placard-carrying Tavua villagers shouted anti-government slogans.

The next day a meeting of the chiefs of the Western Division was held at Veiseisei village (Bavadra's home village): it was called by the Fijian Association, a major constituent of the Alliance party, to discuss the new Government. The meeting decided that the ALTA, which allowed long leases of Fijian land was to be altered by the new government and present leases on Fijian land were to be cancelled.

On the same day, 20 April, 1987, some members of the Fijian Association met behind closed doors at the Raiwaqa Youth Centre in Suva, to discuss the results of the General Election. Reporters and photographers were excluded. A group of Fijians also marched through Suva on Friday, 24 April to present a petition to the Governor-General, Ratu Sir Penaia Ganilau, asking for changes to the 1970 Constitution.

On Tuesday, 20 April, 1987, Prime Minister Bavadra met the Governor General over security and briefed him on the Tavua incidents. He also held an emergency meeting with the Commissioner of Police, Mr. P.U. Raman, about the incidents, and demanded a much tougher stand against those involved. He was not pleased with the way police had handled the situation. In a radio broadcast, Bavadra condemned attempts to destabilise his government, and emphasised that security would be protected by the full resources and power of the law. Such a threat did not go down well with Fijians. They knew that most judges and magistrates were Indians and this incensed them further.

On Friday, 24 April, 1987 an estimated 10,000 Fijians marched through Suva City to Albert Park after receiving approval from the District Officer, Suva, and being advised by the Governor General to observe calmness and peace during the march. A leader of the march, Taniela Veitata, said that the march had nothing to do with any political party, but was a genuine desire by Fijians to control the Government in their own land and no more. (*Fiji Times*, 23 April, 1987, p.2).

The *Fiji Times* of April 25, 1987, put out the headline, "The Big March," and on page 3 samples of the placards carried by marchers which depicted anti-Indian feelings and responses to what Fijians perceived as Indian arrogant attempts to politically control their country. The messages included:

"We Fijians have no confidence in the Coalition"
"Fiji My Fiji"
"Change the Constitution Immediately"
"Out with foreign puppets"
"Fiji belongs to the Fijians."
"K.C. Ramrakha—the deserter shut up."

(This refers to K.C. Ramrakha, a former deputy leader of the NFP, who had emigrated to Australia, but published regular newspapers articles in Fiji).

"Reddy gun, Bavadra bullet."

(Meaning that Bavadra is only the bullet or mouth piece for Indian lawyer, Jai Ram Reddy).

"Fijians have given away so much for so long it hurts."

"Stop this Indian Government"
"Fiji now little India. Say No. Fiji for Fijians".
"We shall not be misled by puppets"
"We came to Fiji with nothing now we have cars houses and country—
which country? Bloodshed."

During Saturday night of 4 May, 1987, Mr Jai Ram Reddy's firm
was fire-bombed by molotov cocktails. A strong detachment of police
including the Deputy Commissioner of Police, was assigned to investigate
and bring the culprits quickly to trial.

Preventing a bloodbath.

Bavadra allowed the Fijian people their democratic right to publicly
show their disaffection to his Indian dominated Government, but he was
determined to use the strong arm of the law to curb any unruly behaviour
directed at his political supporters. Through his continual reference to
the Governor General for whatever action he was to take in relation to
the disturbances, Bavadra showed his insecurity and lack of self-confidence.
He was observed to be panicking. Many Fijians felt a fear of coming
under a police state and of being found guilty in courts which were mostly
presided over by magistrates of Indian descent.

There was also a feeling that the police force would be increased and
the army, which mostly consisted of Fijians, would be disbanded or reduced
to insignificance during Bavadra's reign. Indians had long questioned the
role of the military forces. They felt it was unnecessary and others demanded
50% of the posts in the force for Indians. Due to the fact that few Indians
volunteered for army service, and to the physical and other inadequacies
of those who did, few had been recruited.

It was also feared in some circles that if the police force failed to
control Fijian opposition, Bavadra would call the Fijian dominated army
to help suppress any intended violence by Fijian dissenters to his Indian
dominated Government.

This fear of Fijian dissenters, identified as the *Taukei Movement*, being
posted against Fijians in the Bavadra's camp, and to stop a possible bloodbath, was a major factor prompting the then Chief of Operations of
the Royal Fiji Military Forces, Lieutenant-Colonel Sitiveni Rabuka, to
take over Bavadra's Government by force on 14 May, 1987.

CHAPTER FIVE

In Retrospect

What went wrong

Fiji after all, was the ancestral home of the Fijians; and in the historical order of things whereby Fijians were the first to claim heritage over it, should have the final authority in their own land. They had fought against foreigners who arrived on their shores to exploit their natural resources and tried to take away their land and wealth. Their ancestor chiefs were manipulated and forcibly made to cede their beloved islands to the British Queen Victoria for "protection". During the early colonial period they suffered quietly and even lost many lives in defending their self-respect and integrity from the rather dictatorial and authoritarian rule of the colonial administrators. They revolted against colonial rule but were subsequently brought under control through the use of firearms. Henceforth, however, they were of one mind to put their trust in the British Crown to rule Fiji fairly and justly. They did this in the fervent hope that one day they would be in a much better position to hold the reigns of government in their own country once again.

Fiji, today however, is paying the price which resulted from immigrants from India arriving in Fiji just over a century ago. They made their home in a country which had already been inhabited for nearly 4,000 years by Fijians of Melanesian and Polynesian ancestry.

By the time sugar was found to be the best crop to make the colony of Fiji pay its way, Britain had decided that the Fijian social system of shared communal living in tightly-knit villages, ruled by chiefs, was unsuited to independent farming and plantation labour. The Fijian race also needed to be protected from the encroachments and adverse influences of foreign cultures which had dwindled Fijian population. Indians were therefore brought in as indentured workers and soon became the main sugar farming group. They prospered, their numbers increased and eventually they became the majority community.

Britain, following the established practice of divide and rule, kept the two races largely apart. In the end she wanted us to come together, but only when she decided to pull out of Fiji. There was a separate administration for the Fijians, based on tradition and custom. The Indians were under the central government and had the advantages of acquiring experiences in modern social and political processes. As Indian political demands grew, they were given their own representatives to speak for them in the colonial legislature. Fijians on the other hand continued to be represented by their chiefs, nominated by the Governor in Council from a list of names provided by the Great Council of Chiefs.

All along the Fijians have been tolerant and generous hosts. They lived in fairly harmonious co-existence with the Indians, although anti-Indian sentiments were publicly expressed from time to time through the Great Council of Chiefs. They usually focused upon increasing Indian population and political aspirations. But the voice of calm tolerance normally prevailed.

Fijians also feared Indian domination, and by 1946, they were outnumbered by Indians who then began to use their numerical superiority to assert and demand more political representation in the legislature, to the unhappiness of both Europeans and Fijians. Indeed when independence and democracy was discussed, the Fijian response to the idea of one person, one vote (common roll) was one of suspicion and outright rejection. It meant one thing, domination by the then numerically superior Indians.

International pressure for the country to move to independence made Britain cut the colonial link. The crucial aspect of the pre-independence constitutional negotiations between the Fijians and Indians was the system of parliamentary representation, and the voting formula. The Fijians once again expressed their fears of Indian domination.

The constitution finally adopted, under United Kingdom influence, was a compromise containing a mixture of provisions which reflected the multiracial nature of Fiji, and in particular the differences between the two major communities, Fijians and Indians. The constitution was not democratic in the western sense, although there were some strong elements of the Westminster approach which were largely alien to the traditional Fijian socio-political model. Fijians accepted the constitution demurely out of respect of their leaders.

Indians also reluctantly accepted the constitution which provided special protection for the Fijians, acknowledging their status, and representation of minority groups out of all proportion to their numbers. It is ironic that, after the coups, Indians were seen to be ecstatic about the 1970 Constitution and demanded its reintroduction. Although there was nothing democratic in the discriminatory parts of the 1970 Constitution, Indians were prepared to go along with it because they had then realized that they could manipulate it to their advantage.

The voting method, and the parliamentary seat allocation had by then made it possible for an Indian-dominated Government to be elected. This was not acceptable to Fijians who had all along expressed their fears of Indian political domination in a country in which they should be ruled by their chiefs and other Fijian leaders. They had always selected Indians and Europeans in the Cabinet—there had never been and never would be a Cabinet without them, so while they expect Indians and other immigrant races to join the Government, they certainly did not want them dominating it.

Fijian leadership's call for multiracialism was scoffed at and rejected by Indians. The main exponent of multiracialism was Ratu Sir Kamisese Mara, the main Fijian political leader, and an enlightened paramount chief with liberal views. To those of his own Fijian people who felt there should be more Fijian control, he preached the idea of multiracialism patiently and consistently. According to him, multiracialism, with Fijians and Indians working together for the good of the nation, was the way ahead. He campaigned to break down social barriers against Indians. He tried hard to dispel mistrust of them both in Fiji and in neighbouring nations. The Indians were a part of Fiji and the Pacific, he said, and would play an important role in national life and regional affairs.

In election after election, Ratu Mara and his colleagues took to the campaign trail to win Indian votes. Campaigning in itself was seen as a concession, a major break with tradition in a culture which places great emphasis on respect for chiefs and the dignity of their office. Chiefs are selected by complex processes each within his or her own tribe. The change indicated the trouble and lengths to which the Fijians were prepared to go for a multiracial partnership with the Indians. The arguments the Fijian leaders put to the Indians in the elections were strong: Vote with us and we can then appoint more Indians in the Government and in Cabinet. Vote with us and build up the trust that will provide multiracial harmony, stability and the continued sharing of resources, such as land. Vote with us, and we can all live together as friendly neighbours, caring for each other. Please accept our invitation to join with us the indigenous people, in the great enterprise of building a nation.

These calls for multiracialism fell largely on deaf ears. Greed and hunger for power blinded the vision of Indian political leaders and the direction was set to topple the predominantly Fijian backed Alliance Government of Ratu Sir Kamisese Mara. Ratu Mara himself was criticised by other Fijians for being "soft" on the Indians, but he defended his multiracial policies and still carried most Fijian support and faith with him. However, the pressures to waver from his multiracial policies were enormous.

Fijians saw their positions in other spheres being steadily eroded by the more competitive, individualistic and ambitious Indians. Most felt that they were increasingly becoming second class citizens in their own land. They were losing ground in education. Indians dominated commerce, the professions and the sugar industry. The Fijians clung to their land and their culture as protection against total domination and loss of identity. Even with the land, though, they seemed to be at a disadvantage,for the prime, fertile areas were largely owned by Indians, or by the Crown and leased to Indians, or owned by Fijians but leased by the Native Land Trust Board to Indians. Despite this, Indians were constantly complaining about lease arrangements, demanding longer and longer tenure. How long would it be before they moved to acquire more of the land itself, especially if, as proposed by some Indian leaders, the Native Land Trust Board was reorganised or abolished? It was true there were constitutional provisions to protect Fijian land, but this did not lessen the suspicion and fears of the Fijian people, particularly if the government went to the Indians. Anyway the Government had the power over the Crown land, power to take land for any purpose it declared "public",it would not have returned the Crown Schedule B lands nor would it have granted the fishing rights to the Fijians who initially had customary rights over such resources.

The Fijians also felt culturally threatened when the authority and role of the chiefs was challenged. The chiefs and the people were one. An attack on the chiefly system, or rejection of it by outsiders was tantamount to an attack on the entire Fijian social structure. The Indians showed no signs of cultural assimilation and sensitivity. Most gave the impression of caring little about Fijian culture and social values. They did not understand them, and in private there were patronising reference to the Fijian way of life. At best Fijians were "nice people", friendly, simple and a little lazy. "Jungalis" or savages, naive, foolish and poor were other common epithets. That was a typical viewpoint and there was more than a hint there of feelings of cultural superiority and arrogance.

As the 1987 elections approached it was clear that once again the contest would be largely along racial lines and close. Most Fijians would vote for the ruling Alliance Party, led by Ratu Mara. There were questions about the likely Indian voting trends with the emergency of a Labour Party. Labour, it was felt would syphon off votes from the traditional Indian power-base, the National Federation Party. Many Indians were disillusioned by in-fighting in the NFP and saw Labour as an alternative vehicle for their communal ambitions and a potential means to draw in enough Fijian votes to tilt the balance in their favour.

For a while it looked as though Labour and NFP would split the Indian vote, leaving the way open for Fijians, through the Alliance Party, to form a Government once again. But the political scenario changed again when the Labour and the NFP formed a Coalition in order solely to topple the Government of the Alliance Party.

As a device for winning enough Fijian votes to tip the electoral balance, the Indian leadership selected a Fijian medical doctor, Timoci Bavadra, to head the new Coalition party. The tactic worked and, as expected, enough voted for the Coalition. The NFP/Labour Coalition could only attract a little over 9 percent of the Fijian votes, however, over 90 percent of Fijians stayed with the Alliance or the "Fiji for the Fijians" Nationalists under Sakeasi Butadroka.

When the votes were counted, the Alliance had gained nearly 49 percent of the total votes cast, and the Coalition 46 percent. The Coalition though, had won 28 seats, giving it a majority of four. This meant Fiji had an Indian-dominated minority Government. The Coalition strategy of anointing a Fijian as leader had brought in just enough Fijian votes to edge out the Alliance.

Thus, the delicate balance, maintained largely by Ratu Mara and the Alliance, had been upset. The racial political scales had tipped away from the Fijians. There was a stunned and angry reaction, especially when the composition of the Coalition Government was finally announced. It had 19 Indians and only seven Fijians, all of whom had been elected largely by Indian votes. In other words the Coalition Fijians were not, and were not perceived as true representatives of the Fijian community. They were the front men for the Indians, including the new, and largely unknown Prime Minister, Bavadra.

Many observers and Coalition supporters, meanwhile, were endeavouring to portray the election results as an exercise in conventional democracy. One party had lost, another grouping had won. They argued it happened in other countries as well and constantly, so why all the fuss? A popular red herring was to accuse the Alliance Party leadership of reluctance to give up office—a propaganda line that continues to this day. It was, and is, convenient to talk about party politics and democracy and to try to ignore the racial polarisation for power struggle between the indigenous Fijians, the *Taukei* of the country, and the immigrants, *Vulagi*, the Indians.

Those pushing the "democracy" argument ignore the living reality of Fiji politics. There never had been democracy as it was defined in the West, and power turned on racial considerations and other socio-cultural factors, and not on party political loyalties and ideologies. Fiji "democracy" with its unique and complex voting arrangements, communal provisions and weighted representation, was not really democracy in the Westminister sense. Democracy was an illusion, a facade, a parting whim of a colonial power that had itself only practised dictatorship.

There was an uneasy relationship too between this democratic illusion and indigenous customary politics, beliefs and values, which still played a large part in Fijian communal village life. The two systems were incompatible in many ways. How different they were was illustrated by a reaction from Fijian villagers when their Fijian leaders toured Fiji islands to explain the constitutional changes in the independence period. Villagers could not understand the necessity for an opposition. It made no sense to them to actually pay people to work against the government and against their chosen leaders in Parliament. The fact that the Opposition was Indian introduced a dangerous racial overtone. It took much trust, and patient explaining by Fijian leaders, to gain initial acceptance of this strange new system of politics. Its introduction, however, did not mean the demise of the traditional communal ways. They continued to be observed in most areas of Fijian tribal and communal life.

To the Fijians, the Coalition victory in the 1987 elections seemed like a clever stunt performed with strings, mirrors and "democracy". The end result was that finally the Indians had got what they had long sought— control of the government and of the country. They had acquired the power to do what they wanted and to obtain the greatest possible freedom of action for themselves. This brought them into conflict with the Fijians who had all along maintained that Fiji was theirs and that the power to control it must be in their hands.

The Fijians' sense of insecurity and disillusion was now complete. They felt they had been too generous and accommodating in accepting the Indians as full citizens of Fiji. Relaxed Fijian attitudes and willingness to share and co-exist had helped turn Fiji into a congenial home for the immigrant community.

The Indians leased the best native land, almost all the agricultural Crown leases and owned most of the freehold too. They had most of the businesses, the canefarms, the new homes, the buses and the cars. What had the Fijians received in return? For a start they felt they had been rebuffed politically—that it was the Indians for the Indians.

As the host community the Fijians had reached out to the Indians for many years in the true spirit of the Pacific islanders. But this desire of Ratu Mara and his colleagues to govern in multiracial cooperation with the Indians was not reciprocated or so it seemed. The Fijians saw themselves outnumbered in professions such as the law, accountancy, and medicine (see page 108). Even in the sugar industry, the country's number one income earner, the Fijians felt left on the fringes. Their plight was summed up graphically in two famous observations made some years before the coups. One well-known Fijian politician and community head had said he felt ashamed to walk down the streets of Suva because he could see nothing there owned by Fijians. Ratu Mara himself had told a public inquiry that if the capital burned, all the Fijians would lose would be the record of their debts.

Since independence, only 20 years ago, measures had been introduced to narrow the socio-economic gap, to enable Fijians to compete more effectively. But progress was painfully slow, with much more effort and sacrifice required to overcome cultural, social and commercial constraints. The Indians too often complained about any move by the Government to practise positive discrimination in favour of Fijians. They always demanded equal treatment even though they dominated almost every sector, both private and public.

Meanwhile prosperity for others grew—a prosperity that gave Fiji a reputation as a model for the Third World. One international organisation commented: "Indeed there can be little doubt that there are very few countries in the developing world today that enjoy Fiji's combination of relative prosperity, social harmony and freedom from suppression." These achievements were no doubt attributed in the main to the stability and the policies of governments led by chiefs and other Fijians. It was, however, ironic that the main beneficiaries were Indians, who had once more, in 1987, cast the Fijian leadership aside. Only this time, they had won the government as well.

The Fijians saw this, and the anger began to rise. There was anger too when they thought about the new Prime Minister. Bavadra was unknown, untested, a newcomer to politics. He had come out of nowhere and now he was PM. Many Fijians wondered, in view of Bavadra's lack of credentials, why he was regarded as such a wonderful leader by the Indians? Why were the Indians prepared to have Bavadra as Prime Minister? What was so *acceptable* about Bavadra, and so *unacceptable* about the tried and tested Fijian leadership which had the support of the majority of the Fijians? Fijians could be forgiven for concluding that Bavadra had risen to the top because he was the Indians' man. He was *their* choice, approved and appointed by *their* community.

Ratu Mara, the choice of the Fijians and a successful leader with an excellent track record, had wooed the Indians for years but the figures from the Indian voters were always against him. It was true that a significant percentage of Indians did vote for Ratu Mara (more than Fijians who voted for the NFP/Labour Coalition) but they were always in the minority, and were sometimes cold-shouldered by the Indian masses.

To the Fijians the Indian racial thrust was blunt and unrelenting. Now, finally, it had achieved its objective. It was a matter now for the Fijians, as they saw it, of survival; protection of their way of life, their land, their very identity.

The Fijian cause was articulated and championed by a new grassroots organisation, the *Taukei* movement, which took its name from the *taukei*— owners of the land. Passions and tension rose as the *Taukei* campaigned, and organised protest marches. Some radical elements had plans to disrupt the country by violent means if need be. It became evident there was a revolution unfolding. The new government was reported to be alarmed; Prime Minister Bavadra "shaken".

The revolution came to a head when Major General Rabuka, who was then Colonel in the Fiji Military Forces, staged his military coup on 14 May, 1987, with the objective of defusing the potential for violence and creating a form of government which would ensure political paramountcy for the Fijians in their own land.

As coups go, the Fiji military take-over was mild. It was executed without loss of life, and the coup leader quickly gave the Indian people reassurances of the military's concern for their security. At no stage did Rabuka threaten the Indians or pressure them to leave. He did not want killing or cruelty or property destruction, but as often happens in such a situation and at the heat of the moment, some property destruction by some Fijians in public happened: molestation and beating of Indian political agitators and suspects were committed by some military and police personnel. These were isolated incidents and certainly not a policy of

Colonel Sitiveni Rabuka at a press conference in Suva after he executed the coup d'etat

the security forces. This was evident in that those who committed such felonies were immediately brought to justice. Indeed it was made plain that Indians were welcome to continue living as full citizens in the land which had given them an attractive home, provided they recognised Fijians' deep-seated feelings about their right to political leadership. There was no move to disenfranchise the Indians or even to reduce their parliamentary representation. That was the position also after the second bloodless coup in September, when Major General Sitiveni Rabuka reassumed control to ensure Fijian objectives were not thwarted in the political process then under way.

The Fijians, in fact are still saying to the Indians that they are welcome to join them in building the country; that they will continue to have their citizenship, protection of personal freedom and civil liberties, property ownership, representation in Parliament, religious rights and other constitutional guarantees. However, they are also trying to convince the Indians to understand the Fijians, as the host group which must exercise the ultimate political authority.

A Fijian leader explained the Fijian position this way:

> After the 1987 elections the Fijians were united by a common fear that their community was threatened, that their cherished way of life, their very identity as a race, was at risk, that they had lost political control in their own land with (for them) frightening consequences. Now many people did not want to recognise or perhaps could not recognise—that these were broadly felt emotions of the Fijian people. It was politically convenient for them to ignore these things, to lecture about democracy (and equality), and to cultivate the idea that the poor, hopeless Fijian masses, didn't really have strong feelings and that when they marched in protest they did so in ignorance, being led by the *Taukei* movement. That viewpoint is typical of the attitudes of many who underestimate the Fijians, who patronise them. It shows how poorly informed they are and how their political judgement is lacking.

It has been a great source of unhappiness to many to see Ratu Mara, an enlightened Fijian chief, motivated by a genuine desire to promote harmony and multiracialism, being constantly rebuffed by the majority of Indian voters. His overtures to the Indians cost him heavily on the Fijian side, but this did not seem to be appreciated. It became evident that multiracialism was not going to work—that when it came to the elections Indians would vote the Indian way. Both groups wanted to run the country. The Fijians wanted to maintain their political priority; the

Indians wanted to take control. In such a situation there was no way the indigenous people would permit themselves to be pushed aside. The international community must have some appreciation of the hopes and fears of a small race of people on this earth who are determined not to be submerged by immigrants.

Overseas distortions

As Fiji's interim government grapples with the problems of restoring the economy, bringing back confidence and formulating a new constitution to replace the 1970 document, opponents overseas continue with a propaganda campaign that distorts the true situation. To many people in the interim administration, sections of the Australian and New Zealand media in particular appear to be willing partners in the dissemination of misinformation. Ill-informed, simplistic and often biased reportage on complex issues raises questions about integrity and professional standards.

The following are some of the main propaganda claims, with explanations of the actual position:

Apartheid

There are constant references to apartheid, disenfranchisement and racism. Fiji has been likened to South Africa and Uganda. Such descriptions are ludicrous to those familiar with the Fijian people and the current relaxed atmosphere in the country. The Fijians, as always, are hospitable and friendly, with a genuine tolerance and concern for others. People of all races interact and move freely about. There is no restriction on any race in any place. This attitude is part of a cultural tradition which sets the South Pacific aside from most of the rest of the world. What the Fijians are saying, however, is that although many other cultures and people are free to contribute to Fiji and its way of life, their influence should not become a threat to Fijian traditions—they should not dominate the Fijian way, or supersede it.

The constitution, in essence, has been amended to protect the proud traditions that are the core and essence of being a Fijian. The indigenous people, the Fijians, also want their special position to be made more secure, especially in terms of their right to govern in their own land. Others, as stated, are welcome to play a full role in the running of the country, but with a Fijian majority guaranteed in Parliament. Fijian land rights will be protected and the Fijians expect due respect to be given to their customs and traditional way of life. The new constitution also provides for these matters. Christianity, the religion of the Fijians, is acknowledged in the constitution. Other religions are also free to practice. The new constitution also bestows citizenship on all Fiji's people and it envisages a society founded on respect for the spiritual and moral values of the different communities, with a universal observance of the rule of law.

There is no move to deny Indians a voice in Parliament. They will continue to enjoy a satisfactory level of representation—27 seats, an increase from that provided in the 1970 Constitution, though the Fijians who now hold power could easily deprive them of any representation if they wanted to. In fact the constitution proposed in many ways resembles the 1970 document.

The draft provisions were considered by an advisory committee with members drawn from all Fiji's ethnic groups. It then went to the Cabinet of the Interim Government, and then to the Great Council of Chiefs, the important forum of traditional leaders, before being implemented by presidential proclamation. The constitution embraces all the principles of a free society. It guarantees:

> The fundamental rights and freedom of the individual relating to life, liberty, religion, security of the person and protection of the law. Freedom of conscience, expression, assembly, association and movement. Protection for the privacy of home and property, and security of property ownership.

The Fijians would like to see the Indians continuing to enjoy a full and fulfilling life in Fiji, especially in their traditional role as business people, sugarcane farmers, in the public sector and the professions. Indeed, many of the policies introduced by the administration favour commerce and are designed to encourage Indian businesses to expand, diversify and to improve their profits.

There is continuing recognition of the importance of the Indian contribution to the sugar industry and many measures have been introduced to assist the farmers. In particular the farmers have been given assurances about the legal security of their leases. Marketing of sugar under long-term agreements is aimed at getting a good and stable return for their sugar crop. The best marketing agreements (for sugar and coconut oil with the European Community, Malaysia and others; for manufacturers under SPARTECA with Australia, New Zealand etc.) were negotiated by Ratu Mara personally for the benefit of the Indian community in the main. His personal standing and skill got them a better deal than they would have got otherwise. Indians will continue to occupy important positions in commerce and in the public sector. There are many senior Indian officials, including judges, magistrates and police officers. Most of the country's mayors are Indians, as are most members of town and city councils and their administrative organisations.

Having made the point that Indians have a permanent place in Fiji, with constitutional rights, and freedom to pursue the opportunities offered in a rapidly developing nation, the Fijians are also emphasising that some readjustment is necessary to ensure proper and adequate Fijian participation in the economy. A fuller Fijian role is vital for future stability. Fijians cannot become merely spectators, as the prosperity of others continues to improve. Ways must be found to open up to them sectors of the economy which have until now been virtually the exclusive preserve of other ethnic groups. Although the coups were pro-Fijian they were *not* anti-Indian (a popular misconception) in the sense that they only retrieved to the indigenous Fijians their inherited right to rule in their land. It was no more against the Indians than against any of the other minority groups. And how many Chinese and Europeans do you hear complaining? Hardly any did.

Restraint, discipline, order

There are frequent claims about alleged repression, infringement of human rights and instances of torture by the Army. Most of these claims are gross exaggerations. At one stage a well-organised rumour mill was pumping out wild stories depicting all manner of "atrocities." Harrowing tales were told of "refugees" fleeing to other countries, of multiple murders, random rape and persistent violence. These accounts are now well and truly discredited. They were fabrications, concocted and disseminated in an effort to destabilise the nation by spreading fear and despondency. These fabrications were also meant to get sympathy from Australia, New Zealand, Canada and the United States by those who left and those left behind in Fiji in the hope of acquiring refugee status in those countries. There were no refugees, no random killings (the only killing was an Indian of himself when he was carrying a bomb to set off) and other varieties of mayhem, as described by the rumour mongers. There was probably more destruction and naked violence in the Queen Street riot in Auckland, New Zealand in 1988 than in the entire period of the two coups.

The Fiji Military Forces have a well earned reputation for professionalism and they have won international praise for their role as peacekeepers in the Middle East. All the army's skills and experience were used in the Fiji coups. The leadership demanded high standards of discipline, restraint and tact. Whenever a complaint against the army was registered, a proper inquiry followed. That is still the case. In those instances where personnel were found by the military to have acted in an unacceptable manner they have faced disciplinary proceedings or been dismissed.

It is natural—in view of the coups—for the army to have a much higher profile than usual. That is normally the case when there has been military intervention. Associated security concerns, especially threats from overseas, explain why the government—and the army—were granted additional temporary powers under the controversial Internal Security Decree. The decree was a direct response to a clandestine shipment of arms, clearly intended for use against the government. Special measures were needed to deal effectively with the threat. Comparatively few people were detained under the decrees and the security forces exercised discretion before invoking it. The Army Commander gave his personal assurance that the decree will not be abused. There is no doubt that the Fiji coups were among the most orderly and well-planned in the history of military takeovers. Even the court cases involving the Indian who hijacked the Air New Zealand aircraft, and those accused in the smuggling of arms into the country were judiciously resolved. The fact that no jail sentences were handed out to Indians found guilty is not only a compliment to the justice system but also a testimony for a benevolent government.

An economic boom?

Many media reports, fueled by rumour and planted misinformation, portray Fiji as a land in turmoil. The New Zealand print media in particular have a distorted view of our country. The extent of this was illustrated recently when a New Zealand journalist expressed surprise at the calm and friendly atmosphere in the country. Newspaper stories in New Zealand had led him to expect anarchy, he said. Life in Fiji goes on as normal. Business goes on as normal. Tens of thousands of visitors and other travellers can testify to this.

One Australian development aid expert, Peter Truscott, recently said in a radio broadcast that there was a vibrancy about the country, and it looked as though it was going places. That was typical of the reaction of many who came to the country, with an open mind. The Minister of Finance, Mr Josevata Kamikamica, recently described Fiji as one of the safest place in the world. Another popular pastime of journalists, commentators and opponents of the government is to predict economic ruin. The economy is on the point of collapse, they say, because of recession caused by the coups. In fact most economic indicators point to a strong revival, with numerous expressions of confidence by local and overseas investors. One of Fiji's leading Indian business house recently announced a major expansion programme. Other Indian companies have responded to the government's incentives by investing in new ventures.

There is an unprecedented level of interest by overseas investors, and the Japanese company EIE, recently disclosed plans to spend $400 million on a resort project—the largest, single private development ever in the South Pacific. This project is well underway. Some local analysts, including bankers, are now saying Fiji is on the verge of an economic boom which could create a labour shortage.

Foreign reserves are high (December 1989, F$315,000,000; June, 1990, F$315,000,000), employment figures are improving (1988, 76,000; 1989, 87,000; March 1990, 87,265), and tourism arrivals look good (1988, 208,155; 1989, 250,852; 1990, Estimated 275,000). The sugar industry expects earnings this year of $270,000,000. This is in contrast to 1989 figure of $218,000,000 and 1988 of $209,000,000.

Sunday observance

The government has been criticised for measures relating to the observance of Sunday as the Sabbath. The Sunday observance rules are a reflection of deep and sincere Fijian feelings about the sanctity of Sunday. They are a reflection also of strong Christian traditions in Fijian society, and the desire of the Fijians for Christian principles to be recognised as a major influence in Fiji. The Sunday ban was also intended at one stage as a security measure to discourage gathering in large groups and plotting to destabilise the country. It was during a Sunday evening that some Indians were injured and one killed from a bomb they carried.

A Political Illusion

A common misconception is that the first coup removed a Labour government, and that it was removed because of Labour policies. Fiji did not have a labour administration. It was a coalition grouping which gained its main political momentum from Indian communal ambitions rather than party political ideology. Labour had abandoned its main policies and virtually lost its initial identity, becoming enveloped and absorbed by the National Federation Party, which traditionally attracted almost exclusively Indian votes. The Labour name was unimportant. The party could have been known by *any* name, and still have won Indian support as its membership and leadership showed it was clearly an Indian party, with the acknowledgement that it needed a Fijian figurehead to survive. It was a vehicle, as part of a coalition, for the Indian vote—not a promoter of Labour policies. It is unlikely that Labour would have won more than perhaps 4 seats at all if it had not joined with the National Federation party.

Another myth relates to the so-called "multi-racial" nature of Labour and the Coalition. An impression has been created that the Coalition was the first party in Fiji to win multi-racial backing. The truth of the matter is that the Alliance Party, which commanded majority Fijian support, was much more multi-racial than the Coalition. In 1987, it attracted more Indian votes than the total of Fijian votes that went to the Coalition. The Alliance won the overwhelming support of part-Europeans, Europeans, Chinese and other groups as well.

The Coalition, apart from its solid Indian support, only won just over nine per cent of the Fijian voters and even fewer of those from the rest of Fiji's voting groups. So it had far less representative multi-racial support than the Alliance.

Conclusion

It is important to understand and appreciate the development process through which Fijians have been made to feel helpless, and to lose confidence in themselves and in their ability to determine their own destinies. Through the years of foreign controlled development they have been misled by a number of development ideologies, premises and promises which almost destroyed their sense of direction. They have become confused and dependent by indiscriminately involving themselves in the alien development processes of modernism, individualism and multiracialism which allowed others to undermine their beliefs and values and the respect for their way of life. Through foreign imposition and inculcation of the ideas of democracy and equality, Fijian people's position and rights in their country of heritage have been challenged and eroded.

After being reticent and complacent for so long, Fijians could no longer be kept subdued when they felt threatened by a non-indigenous takeover, unless their rights and heritage were secured in Fijian hands. Negotiations by their chiefs and other Fijian leaders ever since the foreigners arrived on their shores had fallen on deaf ears. The questions about Indian presence in Fiji and their increasing number were often brushed aside in a paternalistic and rather arrogant manner so that Fijians were often placed in an indeterminate state. They felt insecure and threatened in the face of increasing number of immigrants who dominated both the private and public sectors. They became unhappy and very suspicious of Indian political demands and ambition. Fijians were also deeply offended by the Indians' sarcastic remarks and taunting of Fijian inabilities to improve their lot economically and socially. Fijians had been labelled poor and lazy when most never felt that way. Although they had little money, they had plenty to eat and drink with their land and the sea to live upon. Both these resources, however, have been increasingly exploited by others for their financial gain which in turn placed restrictions on their use for Fijian livelihood. Fijian culture, beliefs and values, which emphasised share and care, had been challenged and eroded to the extent that Fijians seemed to be losing everything but gaining nothing.

The Fijian desire to escape from these problems demanded change, and this change inevitably provoked internal conflict which had finally to be resolved through the use of arms, but only after numerous appeals to reason failed. The use of the armed forces to resolve conflict is not new, however unacceptable it may seem. It is the last thing the subdued or dominated resort to when diplomacy fails, and where greed and lack of respect and non-cooperation exist. The Fijians of my home area, the *Colo* tribes, were brought under British rule by the use of military power, and the Europeans of the day applauded our crushing defeat. They did not object to the use of force to secure and protect their position, in fact they insisted on it. Nor has the Government of India been reluctant to use force to maintain power in its own country.

Those who rely upon the democratic process and theoretical equality to advance their interests and exploit the weaknesses of others must understand the nature, direction and control of social forces. They must relate the possibilities and limitations of democracy and the irrational over-emphasis on equality to the urgent demands of the political crises and social situation in Fiji today. They must understand that life, freedom and happiness are bound up with changes in economic and social relations of which respect and cooperation are important elements. Before they place their hopes for further advancement upon the democratic process and on the idea of equality, they must make sure that these ideas will prove adequate to the difficult task of trying to live together harmoniously in a multiracial society.

It is imperative that Fijians must be given a special position in their country and that an element of positive discrimination be practised in favour of them for a period in education, politics, business development and other areas in which they are lagging behind. This must continue until they are at par, with those who have been well established through close contact with colonial and capitalist elites and institutions. Fijians, however, must make great personal sacrifices and work hard if they are to catch up with the others and to continue to control their destiny and their country. Fijians, nevertheless, must be assured of a degree of political paramountcy if all races are to live together peacefully.

BIBLIOGRAPHY

Brewster, A.B., 1922, *The Hills Tribes of Fiji*, J.B. Lippincott Coy., London.

Burton, J.W., 1910, *The Fijian of To-Day*, Charles H. Kelly, London.

Clark, R.R., 1879, *Story of a Little War*, Letters and Notes written during The Disturbances In The Highlands (Known as the Devil Country) of Viti Levu, Fiji, Vol I & II. Privately printed by R.R. Clark, Edinburgh.

Cyclopedia of Fiji, The Cyclopedia Company of Fiji, Sydney, 1907. Reprinted by Fiji Museum, Suva, 1984.

Derrick, R.A., 1946, *A History of Fiji*, Printing And Stationery Department, Suva.

Fish, E.K., 1970, *The political Economy of Independent Fiji*, Reed, Wellington.

France, P., 1969, *The Charter of the Land; Custom and Colonisation in Fiji*, Oxford University Press, Melbourne.

Gillion, K.L., 1962, *Fiji's Indian Migrants: A History to the End of the Indenture in 1920*, Oxford University Press, Melbourne.

Gordon, A., letters to Walter Carew - MS.105A-B, Hocken Library, Dunedin.

Government Reports And Papers, Legislative And Parliamentary Debates Records kept at the National Archives, Suva, Fiji: Colonial Report 1880-83. Legislative Council And Parliamentary Debates - 1943, 1945, 1946, 1947, 1948, 1955, 1956, 1959, 1961, 1962, 1963, 1964, 1965, 1975, 1976. Lord Salisbury Emigration Despatch No. 39 of 1875.

Government of India's reply to the Despatch No. 15 of 1877.

CSO Files — 81/1694, 81/1694, 81/1797, 77/11, 1646/77, 77/12, 77/22, 77/91, 12/2, 12/3, 12/30, 58/30.

Henderson, G.C., 1931, *Fiji And The Fijians 1835-1856*, Angus and Robertson Ltd., Sydney.

Legge, J.D., 1958, *Britain In Fiji 1858-1880*, Macmillan Coy. Ltd., London.

Mayer, A.C., 1963, *Indians In Fiji*, Oxford University Press, London.

Meller, N. & Anthony, J., 1968, *Fiji Goes To The Poll*, East-West Centre Press, University of Hawaii.

Nayacakalou R., 1975, *Leadership in Fiji*, Oxford University Press, Melbourne.

Newspapers: Fiji Times 1873, 1987.

Ravuvu, A., 1972, *Fijians At War*, Institute of Pacific Studies, USP, Suva.

Roth, G.K., 1953, *Fijian Way Of Life*, Oxford University Press, Melbourne.

Routledge, D., 1985, *Matanitu The Struggle For Power In Early Fiji*, Institute of Pacific Studies, USP, Suva.

Scarr, D., 1980, *Ratu Sukuna, Soldier, Statesman, Man Of Two Worlds*, Macmillan Education Ltd., London.

Spate, O.H.L., 1959, *The Fijian People: Economic Problems And Prospects*, Council Paper No.13, 1959, Suva.

Thomson, B., 1968, *The Fijians*, Dawsons of Pall Mall, London.

Wallis, M., 1851, *Life in Fejee, or Five Years Among The Cannibals* (By A Lady) , William Heath, Boston.

Wilkes, C., 1845, *Narrative Of The United States Exploring Expedition During The Years 1838, 1839, 1840, 1841, 1842*. Vol.III, Lea and Blanchard, Philadephia.

INDEX